# The Hate Factory

# The Hate Factory

✦

## A First-Hand Account of the 1980 Riot at the Penitentiary of New Mexico

*Revised Edition*

## *By G. Hirliman based on Interviews with inmate W. G. Stone*

iUniverse, Inc.

New York  Lincoln  Shanghai

# The Hate Factory
## A First-Hand Account of the 1980 Riot at the Penitentiary of New Mexico

iUniverse books may be ordered through booksellers or by contacting:

iUniverse
2021 Pine Lake Road, Suite 100
Lincoln, NE 68512
www.iuniverse.com
1-800-Authors (1-800-288-4677)

First printing—October 1982

ISBN-13: 978-0-595-36669-9 (pbk)
ISBN-13: 978-0-595-81090-1 (ebk)
ISBN-10: 0-595-36669-4 (pbk)
ISBN-10: 0-595-81090-X (ebk)

Printed in the United States of America

*To the end of prison*

# *Contents*

# FOREWORD

*Two Decades After the Riot*

*What is dangerous to all of us now is the distribution of wealth and power in a society where some few people have too much of both and most of us have way too little of either. What is dangerous is creating a climate where many people support treating others in ways we would never believe we ourselves should be treated. What is dangerous is equating justice with punishment and believing that punishment is necessary.*

—Mara Taub, Director, Coalition for Prisoners' Rights [1]

It's a movie set, the old prison! In 2004, a remake of 1974 film "The Longest Yard" was filmed inside the penitentiary. Adam Sandler, Burt Reynolds, Chris Rock, all walked through the halls and cellblocks bloodied in the riot, actors playing inmates and vindictive corrections officers in the belly of the skeleton of the beast. The handball court, which inmates built for themselves after the riot, was torn up to lay turf for the film's football field. The state owns the prison, and does not charge filmmakers for its use. If the governor says ok, you too can shoot your movie at the site of the most savage riot in America's history. New Mexico's Film Commission and tourism department will be happy to take you on a tour of the empty old prison. Just call them on your next trip to The Land of Enchantment and they'll arrange guides to take you through death row and into the gas chamber. Perhaps they will even point out the hatchet marks permanently cut into the floor—maybe where Paulina Paul's head was so agonizingly severed, or where the one-armed man almost lost the other to the blade of a berserk biker. Beware however: there are ghosts in the prison. The movie's location crew heard them, in the first weeks of readying the prison for filming. They heard them when they went into the dark recesses of the basement to death row and the gas chamber. Eerie, they said, a howling like a coyote, or a wounded human. It seemed to be set off by the flash of their cameras. Some of the crew were taking pictures of the gas chamber when, just as the flashbulb went off, the wailing began; everyone there heard it. When told of this, a guard from the old days, now working part time on the movie set as a security guard, related his own eerie camera experience in the gas chamber. It happened when he was working intake in the 80's. The gas chamber, including its several antechambers, had been turned into an intake processing room. In 2004 there were still remnants of that: a vertical measuring 'tape' painted on the wall, signs directing where to stand while waiting. Processing procedure required that the officer photograph each new inmate. One day, the photo he took of an inmate came out fogged. He took another, and another, but they kept getting foggier. He kept retaking the picture and it kept getting progressively foggier. Then, a face emerged. He took more pictures and with each, the face got clearer, until it began fading again into fog, foggier, and nothing. He took the photo first to the mental health department. They were interested enough to try it themselves and took pictures in the same spot, but nothing showed. The old-timer guard then brought the photo to a friend in the records department. She searched the old microfilmed files and drew up a likeness of David Nelson Cooper, the only human to have been killed in the gas chamber. (There had been less killing in the gas chamber than anywhere else in the penitentiary. Aside from Cooper, the only other death in it was that of the pig used to demonstrate the chamber's lethal effectiveness.) The photo of Cooper at the time of his execution had no beard, whereas the face in the guard's photo did. This seemed a logical difference. He likely would have been shaved before his execution, and his spirit, his ghost, would have remembered himself with a beard. The guard put the photos in his locker at the penitentiary and kept them there for a long time. So long that when the penitentiary was at last closed and he moved out of the building, he forgot and left them there, where they were tossed in the garbage by the cleaning crew that cleared out the lockers.

The old riot-torn prison was officially closed Nov. 21, 1998. Three other new and renovated facilities rose up around it—that old brick and mortar, can't get out from under its smell. And what a smell at least two of those edifices contain thanks to new, and stringent, policies and programs:

> The recent implementation of the Level System within the New Mexico Corrections Department requires that inmates who cannot be managed in general population, or cannot function in general population due to criteria established by policy will be separated from the general population. Management of such inmates will be based upon behaviorally based step programs, in which increased privileges are granted for inmates who demonstrate appropriate behavior for a specified period.[2]

Those inmates who "cannot be managed or cannot function in general population" are sent to either the North Unit (Medium/Maximum Custody), or the South Unit (Special Controls Facility) Maximum Security—known more affectionately as Max and Super Max. There is one good change in the design of the brick and mortar, and therefore in the understanding of corrections officials who designed it: there are no more dormitories; everyone sleeps in their own locked cell. Of course, in Super Max, 23 hours a day are spent in there as well. There are no dayrooms, no places to congregate. All meals are served in the cell. The benefit of all this segregation is that there's no getting raped by other inmates, and it sure cuts down on gang revenge. Most of the cells are steel pods, with narrow windows, a bed, desk, stool and toilet bolted down or molded into the pod unit. The doors have a food port and window that the inmate is prohibited from covering for any reason at any time. The Hole in both Max and Super Max is much more hospitable than the dank dungeons of the old penitentiary. It's a cell like any other, shiny and new, with a real toilet instead of a hole in the middle of the floor. Time in The Hole brings an inmate who is deemed a "security threat" 24-hour lockdown, no hour out for exercise and no visits either. Super Max is used as a threat for all prisoners in the system, a place they will be sent for any and all violations, real or trumped up.

The use of Super Max segregation for a new program called Cognitive Restructuring has created fresh controversy. Inmates, their families, and prison reform advocates all have complained, with fervor, about the program and the way it is administered, and the ACLU has filed a lawsuit to stop its use. New Mexico's corrections department describes Cognitive Restructuring as a "…behaviorally based step program, in which increased privileges are granted for inmates who demonstrate appropriate behavior for a specified period of time." What is disturbing, and the root of the ACLU lawsuit, is the use of segregation in concert with this program: if you don't give the right answer, you get more time in lockup. You can go to an online search engine and type in Cognitive Restructuring and get a long list of websites that sell, and tell about, the many uses of Cognitive Restructuring. It is sold as a self-imposed hypnotism for quitting habits, overcoming insomnia and bettering life. Put in a prison situation, where the wrong answer nets an inmate punishment in the form of time in solitary, cognitive restructuring becomes brainwashing. This is what the ACLU claimed: "…One aspect of prison life [is] particularly draconian—a mandatory rehabilitation program with the fundamental goal of changing inmates' thinking patterns…ACLU lawyers have loudly condemned the Cognitive Restructuring program as brainwashing reminiscent of techniques featured in the movie *A*

*Clockwork Orange.* "[3] Public Defenders, who also filed a lawsuit, say the program is "...devoid of any educational content whatsoever. Inmates only progress when they give the 'right' answers to the open-ended essay questions, and...corrections employees encourage inmates to write self abasing essays with religious overtones, which violates inmates' First Amendment rights to free speech."[4] New Mexico is not the only state to use Cognitive Restructuring in their prisons, but it is the only state to combine the program with punitive measures like long-term isolation.

The genius who shaped the Cognitive Restructuring program for prisons is Dr. Stanton Samenow. He believes that people are born criminals. It's not the environment or anything else that makes a criminal: it's in his genes, he's predisposed. Therefore, there's only one cure: reprogramming. "Cognitive Restructuring is a process of changing subconscious thoughts through bringing a person to a conscious awareness of incorrect programming,"[5] a website on life skills explains. Dr. Samenow began applying this process to the treatment of criminals during a study he conducted with criminally insane inmates at St. Elizabeth's hospital in Washington DC. That experience shaped Dr. Samenow's attitude about criminals, which he summed up in a 2004 commentary for *The Washington Times*:

> Some people choose to do evil. From childhood, they reject everything responsible and positive. Their self-esteem depends upon overcoming others by deceit or force. These folks come from all segments of society—poor and rich, illiterate and highly educated, and all races and ethnicities. Until science tells us more, we have no satisfactory explanation for evil. Sociological and psychological determinism offers only more excuses to criminals who have enough of their own.[6]

He did not prove the rehabilitative success of Cognitive Restructuring during his six-year study at St. Elizabeth's, however.

> Of the two hundred and fifty-five participants, most dropped out of the study, thirty completed the program, and only nine genuinely changed by the established standards. In his own estimate, Samenow believes that the habilitative approach would not reach more than twenty percent. Some have argued that Samenow's scientific techniques, from the beginning, are flawed. Demanding that the patients have, and admit to, what Samenow believes is a criminal's personality is not a strongly scientific position...Some have argued that in disregarding all relevant psychological and criminological theories of criminal behavior, Samenow has misdiagnosed the criminal personality...Despite the fact that the habilitative program is only successful with a minority of hard-

core offenders, Samenow has generated significant popularity in his private practice and among others peripheral to the academic world. Law enforcement personnel, corrections, and politicians frequent his seminars to learn how Dr. Samenow recognizes the criminal and seeks to engineer change within the criminal personality.[7]

In Super Max, where inmates are locked up 23 hours a day, sometimes 24, the Cognitive Restructuring "tutorials" are mandatory, a proviso for being unmanageable, for displaying an incorrigible criminal mind, which, of course, must be reprogrammed. How is this restructuring tutorial implemented? A Cognitive Restructuring-trained teacher, who is not allowed to teach anything else to the inmate but Cognitive Restructuring material, is reduced to delivering to each cell xeroxed homework sheets. The inmate is required to read, and write answers to, the questions, as well as to write an essay. Now, let's stop right there. Essay? Half of these guys think essay means *ese*, ('brother' in Spanish); the other half can't read, can't write a complete sentence or string two thoughts together in their minds, no less *write an essay*!

The program's questions are the killers, though. Tilda Sosaya, a prison reform activist and mother of an inmate in Super Max lockdown, has seen many of these homework questions. "The exercise for the day that most intruded upon my mind was a lesson taken from Socrates on suicide and crime. Basically, it proffered the question: what is better, to kill yourself, or to commit that crime you're thinking of. The correct answer is, it's better to die than break the law. And if you don't answer it right, you stay in 23-hour lockup until you do."[8]

Her son told her: "'It's all bullshit…we just tell them what they want to hear.' One homework assignment [he] describes goes like this: Mary is a prostitute with two children. One night, her car is stolen. Mary needs to take her kids to school every day. What should she do? 'They want us to say she should get a real job and save up money for a car, or borrow money from a friend. But realistically, if she's a prostitute, she'd just turn a few tricks to get the money.'" [8a]

And there's no multiple choice to these question, you have to come up with the answer. Fortunately for some, the vent phone system is still in place so the inmate who can barely read or write and wants to play the game can get the answer, though he'll reduce it to his writing and spelling ability. There are no programs offered even to help the Super Max inmates learn how to read and spell. "Conformity is what they want," Sosaya says. "Cognitive Restructuring insists that an inmate believe that all is right with the world and the values of the dominant culture, that it's better to kill yourself than to be a criminal."[9] Perhaps most of society agrees.

Before entering the dangerous world of crime in New Mexico, whether again or for the first time, consider this:

*Cigarettes are outlawed in all New Mexico prisons.*

That's right: no more cigarettes in the joint.

Of course there's a black market, but it's very costly to light up a Marlboro to get you through the night, and there's no way family can send them in. No gifts at all, anytime, are allowed. Visits are no-contact, conducted with a thick window between visitor and prisoner. Families can send a money order so their relative can purchase food and sundries at the commissary, but it's a very expensive commissary: "A can of beans that sells for ninety-nine cents on the outside costs close to $5.99 inside," one inmate's mother complained. Worth it though, because the food continues to be a major source of disgust and complaint. No worms or mold, but also more soy than meat, and no more than three ounces of it. Soy, turkey, and the ever-present baloney are the main protein sources, and the kitchen staff weighs the protein strictly: three ounces per inmate and not a dollop more. Inmates complain they are hungry, the cooks continue to weigh. If an inmate wanted to file a lawsuit about it, he'd have a hard time. There is no law library in Max or Super Max. Inmates can requisition a law book from the one law library that is maintained by the Department of Corrections for the entire system. That is, the inmate can requisition it if he knows the exact title—and law books have complicated titles. Unless an inmate is near some old-timer who has the law books already etched in his mind, jailhouse lawyers won't be popping up in New Mexico's prisons. The library that informed the Duran brothers so they could write what became The Duran Decree—a thorn in the corrections department's side for the 20 years it was in effect—won't be feeding any more hungry minds yearning for a better prison environment.

The demise of the law libraries, the ending of cigarettes, the measured food, the no-contact visits, and so much more, came in with a new Republican governor and his appointed Corrections Secretary, Rob Perry, in 1994. He went one step further than no—contact visits. He instituted video visits. Black and white video. Grainy, the picture fading in and out, video. An inmate is locked up 23 hours a day, has no physical contact, gets two and a half hours a week to visit with people who care about him, and not only can't he touch them, he can only see them in black and white. The visitors have traveled sometimes a hundred miles to see him, and they can't even get a good picture on the screen when they do.

When Perry came into the position of Corrections Secretary in 1994, every-one wanted a hard-ass guy to take the reins. They got that and more. An ex-pros-ecutor and a Republican hard-liner, security was the mantra of Perry's administration, and his use of security was retributive and punitive. "In his first five years in office, Perry made a reputation for himself as a 'get tough on crimi-nals' kind of guy who, at one point in his career, made inmates break rocks."[10] By 1999, Perry had started renovating the medium-security facility on the grounds of the old penitentiary and turning it into today's Super Max, home of "...the worst of the worst,"[11] as Perry described those to be housed there. It was just after the June 2000 opening of the Super Max prison that Perry replaced all of the high-security inmates' programs—computer training, high-school equivalency courses, group therapy—with the Cognitive Restructuring Program. "Even Perry says he knew from the program's inception that he was bound to get sued. After all, the simple words "cognitive restructuring" bring to mind electrodes and hyp-nosis."[12] One Albuquerque lawyer who has participated in lawsuits against the Department of Corrections had no kind words in talking about Rob Perry as Corrections Secretary. "He's a bully. He's contributed to the kind of hatred and feuding that causes prison violence."[13]

In 1999, while Super Max was being worked on and therefore not ready to house the "worst of the worst," there was an event that fired up that bully in Perry: a guard was killed during an uprising at the privately run Wackenhut Guadalupe County Correctional Facility in Santa Rosa, New Mexico. This was the final blow in a year that saw five deaths in Wackenhut facilities. Perry's response was to ship 108 "worst of the worst" inmates out of state to Wallens Ridge State Prison in Big Stone Gap, Virginia. Wallens Ridge, which had just opened in April of that year, was a state-of-the-art maximum-security prison in the middle of nothing but Appalachia's depressed coal mining region. Sent there with the label of "guard killers," these men walked into a nightmare. Letters about racism and torture poured into the inmate family communities and the legal arena. When the families saw the Department of Corrections list of inmates shipped to Wallens Ridge, they were amazed to read the crimes for which these "worst of the worst" criminals had been convicted. "What I discovered was that these were not the 'worst of the worst' inmates, they just happened to live in the same unit where a small group of inmates had a fight. That fight escalated and ended in the very tragic slaying of Officer Ralph Garcia. But not one of those inmates sent to Wallens Ridge has been indicted in that killing...Only a very small percentage could be perceived as some of the worst...the vast major-ity...were convicted of far less serious crimes...None of these men was classified as a high security inmate."[14] This is what some inmates wrote home about their treatment at Wallens Ridge:

> ...Looking out of the bus window we could all see an assembly of about thirty to thirty-five guards, all dressed in black jungle-type fatigue pants and black shirts...The captain...proceeded to yell at all of us that this was their prison and that here they ran it and here we will kill you if you step out of line or touch an officer. Then he held up what looked like a walkie-talkie and said this is the Voltran 2000. He turned it on and it sounded truly electrifying, and said, do the wrong thing and this is what you get. And in the last twenty-two days I've come to learn that all of these guards carry stun guns, and use them at their own discretion...Once I entered the cell I was being led to, I was surrounded by three to four guards. One of these guards grabs me from the neck and squeezing it starts whispering in my ear, are you one of them dirty little Mexicans who killed the guard?" I said, no sir. And he said, you're a lying little stinking Mexican—we were told by your warden that you were. I stated that I wasn't at that prison, and he started telling me, do you know what we're going to do to you here? I said, no sir. And he whispered in my ear, we're going to kill you, here we shoot Mexican trash...He then punched me in the chest and all of them standing around started beating and kicking the hell out of me. I fell to the floor and they shocked me with the stun gun...I was then...lifted into the air and slammed into the steel rail of the bunk, when I fell to the floor. I was shocked again with the stun gun...All that I have just described happened in the first thirty to forty minutes of our arrival there.

> ...I was already falling to the floor and both officers picked me up and pushed me into the wall...and spread my chains again...As I'm up on my toes, the officer said, I'm going to fuck you right in your asshole, boy, when I hit you with this electric gun you won't feel a thing. They were resting the gun on both sides of me, one on my left arm, one on my right. All I know is that I was...buck naked, not anything on me, only chain on my ankles and on my wrist. Four officers were pulling each side of me and I see one man in the middle of me, I said, Hey, man, you can't do that, and at that same time both officers put their electric gun on my side, You shut your fucking mouth, just turn your head, did you hear me, I said turn your head. Then another officer said, Grab your butt cheeks, joking and laughing, you're not going to feel a thing. Which I did feel some one feeling or poking me.[15]

There were many letters describing similar abuse. The families receiving these letters were devastated and outraged. They formed a coalition—COPA, Committee On Prison

Accountability—and worked together to address the Department of Corrections and the legislature to bring their kin home. It kept them busy, but didn't win their cause. Perry wasn't listening. He was too busy with his prime agenda: the building of more prisons, most especially the Super Max.

Many of the New Mexico inmates sent to Wallens Ridge filed a civil rights lawsuit. The lawsuit charged that their fundamental Constitutional rights were violated, in a setting the attorney, Paul Livingston, compared to a "concentration camp." He hoped success in his suit might "help shut down this supermax facility, and others like it across the country, which indeed implement fascist-like treatment of prisoners as routine practice in the United States. Secondly, a successful suit would help to expose the horrors of Virginia's criminal justice system, which is becoming a model for those who would eliminate rehabilitation altogether from prisons and expand even further the 'prison-industrial complex…'"[16] About New Mexico's Department of Corrections, the attorney had an interesting anecdote. "To this day, the New Mexico Corrections Department is saying 'nothing happened; these people weren't mistreated; we have absolute confidence in the Virginia Corrections Department and what they've done to them.' And they've given out little, what prisoners call 'merit badges,' to them, they come as little badges with the New Mexico logo on them or something, and given them out to the Wallens Ridge guards…for the wonderful work they're doing in the prisons!…Our Corrections Secretary, Rob Perry, actually purchased a pile of rocks for the prisoners to spend time breaking up…But there was such a public outcry against it that they still have the pile of rocks, apparently; they haven't gotten any prisoners to break them up."[17] Amnesty International even turned their eyes toward Wallens Ridge. They looked at the allegations of abuse made by the New Mexico inmates and others, as well as the use of stun guns and the conditions in supermax facilities in general. "Amnesty International…is concerned that many aspects of the conditions in supermax facilities violate international standards, and in some facilities conditions constitute cruel, inhuman or degrading treatment. Prisoners typically spend between 22 and 24 hours a day confined to small, solitary cells. Prolonged isolation in conditions of reduced sensory stimulation can cause severe physical and psychological damage."[18]

Perry's imperative for prison expansion embraced not only the super max concept, but prisons-for-profit too. As a result, New Mexico has eight private prisons, joining the movement in post-millennium America to turn our prisons over to private, for-profit corporations. In 2004, a figure emerged that connects New Mexico's old state way and new private way of running prisons with the Abu Ghraib prisoner abuse scandal in Iraq. Lane McCotter, the man who was put in charge of reopening the Abu Ghraib prison, spent four years as Corrections Secretary in New Mexico, from 1987 through 1991, and a decade later, in 2001, came back to manage the private, for profit Santa Fe County Detention Center. When Corrections Secretary Lane McCotter began running New Mexico's prisons in 1987, he had to operate with the federally mandated Duran Consent Decree—designed to improve conditions following the 1980 riot—looking over his shoulder. Frustrating as that was, it didn't stop McCotter from putting his brand of corrections philosophy on his tenure.

> By 1988, already chafing under the Duran decree's federal supervision, McCotter was accused of covering up the abuse of a prisoner. Cuffed and shackled, the prisoner was allegedly beaten by guards and repeatedly slammed against a wall. Federal Court Special Master Vince Nathan requested the videotape of the incident as part of his ongoing supervision of the state's prison under the Duran decree, but the section that contained the alleged beating had been erased. McCotter maintained that the erasure was an "accident" and that the federal prison monitor was 'fabricating atrocities.' Mark Donatelli, one of the attorneys in the landmark Duran case, has said that McCotter disdained oversight and felt that the prison conditions were "nobody's business"—not even the federal court's....Donatelli characterized McCotter's tenure as "oppressive and abusive."[19]

It would not be the last time the words "oppressive" and "abusive" would be used to describe the wake McCotter leaves behind him. In 1992, McCotter left New Mexico to become corrections director in Utah. Near the end of his tenure, in 1997—and many say, the cause of his leaving the job—"a 29 year old schizophrenic inmate...was stripped naked and strapped to a restraining chair by a Utah prison staff because he refused to take a pillowcase off of his head. Shortly after he was released some sixteen hours later, [he] collapsed and died from a blood clot that blocked an artery to his heart...Director of the Utah Department of Corrections, Lane McCotter, who was named in the suit [the man's family filed against the Utah Department of Corrections] and defended use of the chair, resigned in the ensuing firestorm."[20] Shades of Marc Orner in the old penitentiary! McCotter didn't resign quietly. In explaining the use of the chair, he gave the stock reasoning of all corrections officials when confronted with abuse: "We have to have some way to control unruly inmates."[21]

It was four years after this, in 2001, that McCotter returned to New Mexico under the umbrella of the private for-profit prison management company, Management & Training Corporation (MTC), a Utah-based company. (Look at that: the company was in the very state in which McCotter had been successfully sued in for lethal mistreatment of a prisoner, and still they employed him!) They employed him to finalize MTC's three-year contract with the County of Santa Fe and run the Santa Fe County Detention Center. Run it he did, straight to hell.

On McCotter's watch, MTC has been at the center of many prison and jail problems in New Mexico. In September of 2003, MTC lost its contract with the McKinley County Jail after a series of problems, including the escape of four prisoners. MTC continued to run the Santa Fe County Detention Center, even while allegations of abuse and neglect brought a team of U.S. Justice Department experts into the jail to investigate possible civil rights violations. In March 2003, they issued a report concluding that"...certain conditions violated inmates' constitutional rights, and that inmates suffered 'harm or the risk of serious harm' from, among other things, woeful deficiencies in healthcare and basic living conditions. The report documented numerous and horrifying examples, and threatened a lawsuit if things didn't get better. Amid the fallout, the Justice Department pulled its approximately 100 federal prisoners out of Santa Fe and MTC fired its warden..."[22] People who haven't been to trial or declared guilty spend time in County Detention, waiting for their day in court. In such a situation, they definitely feel like victims of cruel and unusual punishment. In July of 2003, just four months after these Justice Department findings, six defendants—one of them a guard—were charged with smuggling drugs into the same MTC facility in Santa Fe. One month earlier, a guard had been put on leave after a female prisoner told police she'd been sexually assaulted on more than one occasion. This brought another Justice Department investigation into the Detention Center, which again found medical neglect, lack of mental health care, as well as easy access to illicit drugs, filthy conditions, allegations of abuse, and lack of educational services at Santa Fe County Detention.

During the time the Justice Department was checking out the Detention Center for the second time, a surreal thing happened. "While [McCotter] and his company were under investigation by the Justice Department, the department's chief, Attorney General John Ashcroft, hand-picked McCotter to 'rebuild' Iraq's criminal justice system (NY Times). Inhale that: Ashcroft selected a man his own department was investigating, a man who had to leave the top corrections post in Utah or face scrutiny for what can only be called torture."[23] Of course, prison reform activists have nothing good to say about McCotter, but "Chase Riveland, former secretary of corrections in Washington and Colorado, who...is respected both by prison reformists and corrections administrators, turned down an offer to join the Justice Department's team. 'The philosophies of the individuals that were going did not match mine.'"[24] The Attorney General's office didn't offer an explanation of how or why a man with McCotter's history was chosen to manage a prison in Iraq. Senator Charles Schumer (D-New York) wanted one, and called for an investigation to find it. "Why Attorney General Ashcroft would send someone with such a checkered record to rebuild Iraq's corrections system is beyond me," Schumer said. "You just don't send someone about whom so many questions have been raised to handle such a sensitive task. It defies logic and reason and it demands answers."[25] McCotter naturally defended himself, putting out a statement denying that he had anything to do with training guards or in any way teaching them to torture and degrade the prisoners held in Abu Ghraib. He denies it, but still, our government knowingly exported abusers of power and civil rights in our own prison system and gave them the job of setting up a wartime prison on foreign soil. (McCotter went to Abu Ghraib with three other corrections professionals, all with similarly abusive records.) "It would seem that McCotter was chosen not in spite of his record but because of it. It's likely that Ashcroft and Wolfowitz, and the people they report to (Rumsfeld and Bush), knew exactly who they were hiring and what was expected of him. It was McCotter who, in the parlance of The NY Times, 'directed Abu Ghraib prison in Iraq last year and trained the guards.' The guards McCotter trained did the infamous things, took the infamous photographs. What did Ashcroft say when he appointed McCotter? This: 'Now all Iraqis can taste liberty in their native land, and we will help make that freedom permanent by assisting them to establish an equitable justice system based on the rule of law and standards of basic human rights.' Orwell would chortle."[26]

The 2001 elections saw the end of Republican Governor Gary Johnson's eight-year administration, and the end of Rob Perry's reign as Corrections Secretary. Perry decided to run for Attorney General, but lost to a Democrat, and a woman, Patricia Madrid. He is rumored to be working on the other side of the criminal justice table, as a defense attorney. Incoming Governor Bill Richardson, a Democrat, and his new Corrections Secretary, Joe Williams, stopped the harsh video visits as one of their first actions, in February 2002. Now, visits for Max and Super Max inmates are face to face, albeit while "separated by a sheet of Plexiglas, which Williams says is to 'prevent the passing of contraband'...Tilda Sosaya, a prison-rights activist who has a son at the maximum-security North Facility...praised Williams' decision. 'It's the first time I've seen my son face to face in two years...It just lifted his spirits. He said it's lifted the spirits of all the inmates. I don't think Joe Williams could have taken another measure that would have had such a widespread effect.'"[27] The ACLU agreed to put the Cognitive Restructuring lawsuit on hold to give the new administrations of Bill Richardson and Joe Williams time to get their bearings and learn about the issue. Family coalitions were feeling more positive about Corrections under Bill Richardson and Joe Williams. "I haven't seen any real changes yet, but I feel safe there's a shift in the philosophy," says Tilda Sosaya. "It couldn't have gotten any harsher than it was. Anything is better than Rob Perry."[28]

It will take a big shift, a shift that begins with the unthinkable therefore unasked question: does punishment work? The history of the biggest punisher, prison, proves it does not. It works to create people you don't want standing next to you in elevators, but it doesn't work to create a better human being, or to deter crime. Consider the meaning of the word *punish: to subject to a penalty for an offense, sin, or fault.* Root: *kwei=to pay, atone, compensate.*[29] So we made penal(ty) colonies, penal systems, penal codes. Guess what: prison is an inefficient penalty. It's time to think up a new one.

### E-mail your idea for a new penalty to:

*hatefactory@writerinthewindow.com*

# 1

*Brutalization begets brutalization, violence begets violence. In Santa Fe we had a system of penology with a mentality that was all punishment. When you take everything away from a human being including his personal dignity, he has nothing left to lose. He becomes extremely dangerous.*

—Dr. John Salazar, former Secretary of Corrections, State of New Mexico [1]

## Friday, February 1, 1980.

There was a full moon that Friday night. I watched it move across the patch of sky framed by the window near my bunk, noticing how it turned the desert surrounding the penitentiary ghost white. I even thought about all the superstitions connected with the full moon and something I'd read recently about a survey proving that crime really did increase every month when the moon was full. I was tuned in, but not enough. It didn't cross my mind that the instigators of a long-planned riot would choose this night to put their scheme into action. Maybe that's because I didn't really think of a prison uprising as something criminal. To me it was a righteous and overdue response to years of abuse, mental and physical. All that overdue rage, though, made people go crazier than anyone expected.

## 11:45 PM.

Eight well-juiced inmates sat around the table in the dayroom of Dormitory E-2. Since just after the 8:30 evening headcount they'd been chugging down a new batch of home-brew, prison booze made of fermented raisins, yeast, sugar and water. Angry and loud, they were bitching about conditions.

"Unless somethin's done soon, The Man's gonna have all the white bros locked down in 3. Over half the brotherhood's in there already," a ranking member of the Aryan Brotherhood told the group. Most of the Anglo population, a minority in this Chicano-dominated prison, belonged to his clique.

"It ain't just you guys. There's a lot of homeboys in lockup right now too," said a lieutenant of the Chicano clique. There was occasional racial tension between the Anglos (the name given to whites in New Mexico) and Chicanos, but usually the two groups maintained a truce and banded together to fight the blacks, none of whom lived in this dormitory.

"So what are we gonna do about it?" another broke in. "We've been talkin' about a riot for so long now—I'm fuckin' tired of waitin'."

"Okay. What about tonight?"

The eight men sat stunned for a moment, then, nodding agreement, grins spread across their faces.

"Well *all right*, that's what I want to hear!"

They poured another round of brew, toasted their decision, and began discussing the details of the takeover. A Chicano leader spoke for his clique. "If we can pull it off, we can count on at least three hundred of our people to back our play. How many white brothers can we count on?"

"At least a hundred and fifty, maybe more. If we can take Cellblock 3, there's another sixty in there."

"I don't trust the blacks. What do you guys think?"

"They're either with us or against us. If they won't go along, we'll fuck them up. But I think they will. They're as tired of The Man's action as we are. In fact, I don't think we're gonna have any trouble getting' the majority of the population to go along with us."

"Okay, let's get the show on the road then. We'll take them when they come in for the 1:30 count, like we planned. I'll call the white bros here, you go get your guys," the Aryan told the Chicanos at the table. "If anyone's asleep, wake the fucker up."

Less than ten minutes later, all sixty-two residents of Dormitory E-2 were crowded into the dayroom, the area usually used for TV watching and card games. These inmates had also been drinking and were well psyched for the instructions being circulated in hushed voices.

"When the pigs come in tonight to take the count, we're gonna grab them and take over this prison. Here's how it's goin' down. When the two screws who're countin' get to the back of the dorm, three of us will grab them."

"Two of us will take the pigs at the door, which'll be easy since these assholes never lock it like they're s'posed to."

"Look asleep when they come in, but be ready to cover our action when we need you. Anyone who stays in the sack after the shit hits is in trouble."

## 1:30 AM, Saturday, February 2, 1980.

Shift Captain Gregoria Roybal and Corrections Officers Michael Schmitt and Ronnie Martinez arrived at E-2 to close down the dayroom and take the final count for the night. Officer Martinez opened the dormitory door and Roybal and Schmitt walked into the unit. Officer Martinez waited outside. Just as Martinez was closing the door, Lieutenant Jose Anaya unexpectedly arrived. He'd received word that there had been drinking going on earlier and decided to come down to back up his fellow officers in case trouble was brewing. He followed Captain Roybal and Officer Schmitt inside E-2. Officer Martinez, as anticipated, did not lock the door behind them, but left it ajar.

Two of the riot planners were lying in wait on bunks by the door and two others were on end bunks by the dayroom. All the planners had homemade shanks (knives) within easy reach under pillows or blankets. When they saw there were three guards instead of the anticipated two, they felt only a moment of panic before one of them whispered to the man in the next bed, "Pass it on: *Everyone* jumps when we make our move. Get ready." They let Schmitt make it to the dayroom, lock the door and turn off the dormitory lights. The leaders knew this would be to their advantage. The only illumination in the place would then come from the bathroom. The blue night-lights used from lockup to daybreak were out of order.

Those lights had been out of order for over a month, though a guard had written a memo requesting they be fixed for security reasons. Rumors of a riot had reached the administration's ears back in mid-January, and its promoters were known to be in E-2. Since then, the officers were more tense than usual when taking final count in that unit. Even if a riot had not been in the wind, corrections officers would have had reason to be wary. E-2 was a minimum-security unit, but just before Thanksgiving it was filled with the most hardcore convicts in the penitentiary. They'd been transferred from Cellblock 5—where the violent, escape-prone, high security risk inmates were permanently housed—so that renovations could be made in that cellblock. It must have been eerie for the guards to walk down the long aisles, dark without those blue lights, especially because the unit was a minefield of double bunks jutting out from both walls and single beds taking up two rows in the center.They knew how easy it would be for an inmate to hide behind one of the double bunks and jump them.

When Schmitt came out of the dayroom, Captain Roybal was halfway down the right aisle and Lieutenant Anaya was four or five bunks in. At that moment all their fears came true. One of the inmates in front sprang from his bed and pushed open the front door while another lunged at Officer Martinez outside, who was struggling to force the door shut. Two men in the back of the dormitory took on Schmitt, and groups in the middle seized Captain Roybal and Lieutenant Anaya. They were all easily overpowered. Captain Roybal and Lieutenant Anaya were both fifty-two years old, short and not particularly physically fit. The convicts were younger and quicker, and most of them spent a lot of time lifting weights. Only Officer Schmitt had the youth and size to be a challenge, but the sheer number of his opposition brought him down.

The four guards were dragged into the dayroom, stripped naked, their ankles bound with torn bed sheets and their hands tied behind their backs.

"Blindfold 'em, too," someone yelled, fastening a canteen-issued bandana tightly around one of the hostage's eyes. "Let's keep these sorry motherfuckers shittin' in their pants. They won't be able t'see nothin', they won't be able to protect themselves. It'll be just like sittin' in the goddamn Hole, hey, pigface? Just like all those times you wrote up tickets on me and sent me into that black pisshole in the basement. Well, it's your turn now, cocksucker."

Using this long-imagined opportunity to pay back The Man, the inmates took turns kicking, punching, spitting, stomping, even pissing, on each of the guards, taunting them with obscenities and threats on their lives and their families.

While these beatings were in progress, one of the riot leaders put on Captain Roybal's uniform and, with about ten inmates, went to find the other four officers they knew were working the south side of the penitentiary. Everyone in this group had a weapon of some kind, pipes or shafts smuggled from various prison shops then stashed in one of the many ingenious hiding places convicts manage to contrive during their abundant idle time. They went downstairs—E-2 is a second-floor unit—pushed open the unlocked riot control grill and stealthily walked the main corridor until they reached the next two dormitories, which were opposite each other. Seeing no guards in them, they headed upstairs to the top tiers and found what they were after. Officers Elton "Bigfoot" Curry, Juan Bustos, Victor Gallegos, and Herman Gallegos (these two were not related) had just locked down A-2 and were about to enter the dormitory across the hall when the weapon-wielding band of rioters came up from behind and grabbed them. Bustos and Victor Gallegos were easily overpowered, but Curry, nicknamed "Bigfoot" for his size, put up a fight, knocking down several inmates before someone stabbed him in the ribs and back. The convicts now had three of these guards under their control. The fourth, Herman Gallegos, had managed to run into the dormitory dayroom. In the hurry to secure their captives, the rioters didn't go after the officer but counted on the residents of the unit to take care of him. They did, but not in the way the rioters expected. Gallegos was lucky enough to find some sympathetic inmates who hid him for the duration of the uprising.

The inmates brought the new hostages down to the E-2 dayroom, where they stripped, bound and blindfolded them as they had the first four guards, then threw them into the middle of the room. It was these seven guards who suffered most at the hands of the rioters. They were the first captured and the first target of the population's exploding rage. When the convicts looked at their old oppressors lying there naked and helpless, some of them crying in fear, the memories of the maltreatment these screws had forced on them flashed through their minds.

Not every one of the seven had been overtly abusive in carrying out his duties, but three of them had. One specialized in finding subtle ways to play with a man's mind. A favorite stunt was to hold back an inmate's mail for a couple of hours. Before he'd deliver it, he'd read it and then come down to tell the dude what was in the letter. This would infuriate the con, especially when it was from his old lady and was filled with personal sentiments that gave him comfort when read privately but sounded embarrassingly asinine coming out of the guard's snide mouth. This officer was also part of the administration's "goon squad," that group called upon to beat an unruly inmate into submission before he was thrown into the Hole. This was also the main gripe against the other two. Many of the hardcore inmates in this group of rioters could remember days of pain in their lower back caused by the Billy clubs of these three guards. They'd never forget being taken to the Hole, hands cuffed to the bars behind them while they were throttled in the kidneys. That's how the goon squad worked—by hitting in the kidneys and back, so no marks would show. These were the guards that were sodomized. Using their cocks like weapons, the rioters paid back The Man with the worst humiliation they knew. They did it in 'trains,' four or five inmates lining up in front of each of the three guards, ejaculating quickly, as if their semen were bullets. They worked up to such a frenzy that eventually their cocks wouldn't do. They had to take a two-foot Billy club, grease it down (only because they tried it dry and couldn't get it in), and shove it as high as they could up one guard's anus. But they didn't kill them: dead guards don't talk about the horrors of payback. They wanted these guards to live with what had been done to them, they wanted to inflict the same kind of suffering the officers had inflicted on them, the kind inmates lived with day by day. And they had the sense to remember that live hostages gave them bargaining power.

When this orgy wound down, the riot leader, wearing the Captain's uniform, went with a few inmates to unlock the other dormitories on the south side, which was now in their control. Using the keys taken from the captured guards, the men unlocked the grills to both tiers of each unit, announcing as they entered, "Okay, loosen up, this is a riot. The white bros and Chicanos from E-2 have take all the screws on this end of the joint hostage. We're gonna take the rest of the place, too. We're in charge now, not the pigs, so let's go!"

Within fifteen minutes some five hundred inmates were turned loose on the south side of the penitentiary. They armed themselves with legs broken off metal tables and beds, knives, razors, broken jars, locks strung on belts, anything they could use as weapons, tearing the dormitories apart in the process.

Only two units on that side were still filled with inmates. One of these was Dormitory D, for which the captured guards had no keys. The other was E-1, a semi-protection unit for younger men whom convicts had tried to rape. These men turned down the freedom the riot offered and instead barricaded themselves in the dormitory with chairs, tables and beds rammed against the steel door. They had the right idea. The beatings the first seven guards took would seem humane compared to the sadism the rioters would act out in the next thirty-six hours. This was destined to become the most savage prison riot in America's history.

# 2

*So we're all even, right? I did it, I'm here for doing it. Fair and square, no complaint. Paying for my debt to The Man. But brother, you got to understand that's just the way it ought to be, that's not the way it is. That Man is committing crimes against me every day I'm here. And nobody's saying shit about that.*

—Inmate, Attica State Prison [1]

Why does a person become bitter when they're in prison? How can you avoid it when the people running the show have nothing in mind but punishing you; when there's no sign of humanity or intelligence shown by those whose job it is to "rehabilitate" you; when society refuses to pay attention to what goes on inside the institutions it shoves its aberrants into; when politicians refuse to allot to such an unpopular cause the money needed to hire adequately educated personnel? And the roots of the bitterness aren't cut off when a convict gets out of prison on parole, either, at least not in New Mexico, "Land of Enchantment." They've enchanted themselves into believing that a parole officer can take on a caseload of 150 parolees and give the individual supervision needed to help the ex-convict readjust to life on the streets without returning to his old criminal ways. Under the circumstances, the parole officer does the best he or she can, which isn't very "best" at all. "Stay out of trouble, see me once a month, and make out your report," my parole officer told me. "If you're busted, you go back to prison." In short, don't make any waves for me and I won't make any for you.

I made waves. That's how I ended up back in the joint two months before the February riot. It was a bum rap. I tried to explain the circumstances to my P.O., but she was more concerned with appearances than facts. It didn't matter to her that I was innocent of the rap I was picked up on, or that I was holding down a good job and thereby demonstrating my desire to "reform" and stay out of trouble. What mattered to her was that I'd made her look bad by getting fingered. In her mind, where there's smoke there's fire, so back you go, let the parole board decide whether the charges were true or not. She wasn't going to take any responsibility beyond the prejudices she'd formed because I was an ex-con.

Maybe, like my P.O., you figure: bum rap, my eye, once a con always a con. That's what most people think, that's why getting a job when you're out on parole is a bitch: very few want to risk hiring an ex-felon. So what's a parolee going to do? He's still got to eat and he's still got to find some goodies in life. He's out of money, his P.O., who theoretically is supposed to help him through the difficulties of re-entering mainstream society, has too big a work load to care or pay attention. Naturally, he turns to his only friends, ex—or soon-to-be con-victs, and the only livelihood he knows. *Whammo,* he's back in the clink.

I was lucky. As I said, I had a job, a good job. The halfway house I'd been paroled to hired me as the maintenance man for $250 a week. My P.O. was all for me the first four months. Every time I'd go in to see her, she'd tell me how well she thought I was doing. She knew that some of the ex-cons who'd also been paroled to the halfway house worked for me, which meant I was technically vio-lating one of the sacred clauses of the parole contract: no association with ex-fel-ons.

One night I did a co-worker—an ex-felon—a favor and drove him to a friend's house. His friend wasn't there, but the girl who answered the door said she'd show us where to find him. We drove around with the girl for a few hours, stopping at several places but never locating the dude. Finally, at about one in the morning, we gave up and took the girl home. As luck would have it, her mother met us at the door, in a rage that her daughter had been out so late. The girl was not the twenty-year-old she looked to be, but a jailbait fifteen. We were happy to drive away from this scene, but the next day we found out there was more to come.

To cover her action, the fifteen-year-old told her mother we'd raped her. Mother and daughter had traipsed down to the Rape Crisis Center the following morning to tell the tale. A warrant was issued for our arrest. When I heard about it, I turned myself in to show that I had nothing to hide. I explained to my parole officer that there was nothing to the charge, I was innocent, and she said, "If you can beat the rap, I'll release you." I breathed a little easier as I sat stewing in the county jail, waiting for the Grand Jury to hear the evidence against me. When they did—a month later—there was no evidence. The girl had not only left town: the medical report showed that she hadn't had sexual intercourse for at least forty-eight hours prior to the time she'd been tested. The Grand Jury refused to indict me, and the rape charge was thrown out. I beat the rap, but my P.O. had changed her mind about releasing me. She couldn't keep me locked up on the original charge because it had been dropped. She found a new one that would automatically revoke my parole: associating with an ex-felon, a horseshit charge if I ever heard one, given that she knew all along my job was at a parolee halfway house where I worked side by side with ex-felons.

I think the word *rape* freaked her out. Believe it or not, I'm all for equality for women, and I'm sure there are as many good female parole officers as there are male, but I don't see the point in having a young, inexperienced woman counseling a forty-year-old man who's spent the last fourteen years behind bars relating only to hardened male criminals. I hadn't been near a female in so long I hardly knew how to act with them when I got out. How in hell was I supposed to go to her with the problems I was going through, for instance the impotence that hit me for the first two months after my release, not an uncommon complaint for male parolees? And in fairness to my P.O, how was she supposed to understand where I was coming from? To her, I was a dangerous criminal and the smoke of the rape charge meant fire to her. She told my old lady, who'd gone in to plead my case, that she believed I'd done it even though the charges were dismissed. "He should be locked up, he'd be better off in prison. He'd be away from society and society would be protected," she said.

She revealed much more of her true attitude about her clients, and me, in that conversation with my old lady. "Two of my other clients have been arrested, and it really bothers me that my clients keep breaking the laws like this, making me do extra paper work and giving me these headaches. I got called on the carpet to explain why so many of my clients were doing so poorly. They make me look like I'm not doing my job well." She went on to say that she was afraid of people like me. To her, I was exactly like one of her other clients, a man who'd just gotten arrested for raping his wife—with a hot curling iron! "Wally is in the same class with him," she wound up. "You might as well kiss him goodbye, because he's going back to the penitentiary where he belongs."

And so I went. I had a preliminary hearing before a hearing officer, but I knew that this officer, also a woman, would act on my P.O.'s recommendation, which she did. Still, this wasn't the final ruling; that was reserved for the three-member parole board itself. Until they could find the time to hear my case and rule on whether I was fit to reenter society, I had to spend more time in the overcrowded, cockroach-infested penitentiary where I'd already lost fourteen years of my life.

It was a cold, gray, December Monday when I walked through the prison gates, and my mood was as bleak as the weather. The street clothes I was just getting used to wearing were taken from me by the admitting officer and put in an envelope. In their place I was given the drab green prison uniform I'd worn for so many years. I was assigned to C-1, the "old men's dormitory," where the old-timers who couldn't cope with the madness of the general population were housed along with guys like me who were either doing short time on parole violations or waiting for a hearing.

Like every other unit in the institution, C-1 was overcrowded. Built to house forty inmates, I was the forty-eighth. There were no more single beds available, so I was assigned an upper bunk. I'd gotten spoiled in my six months out—I was used to sleeping on a firm bed. This one tore me apart. Even in the county jail the mattress hadn't been so thin. I could feel the metal springs of the frame, and they sagged so much that my spine ached after my first night's sleep, what little of it I was able to get. During the next few days I found out that my own anger at being back in this hellhole matched the resentment that was seething in my old friends.

My fellow inmates were ready to move against The Man. In fact, they'd planned to grab hostages and take over the place just before I arrived, but a snitch had gotten wind of the details and told the administration, so the scheme was postponed. Not called off, however. Things were too oppressive in the penitentiary for the men to forget about making their troubles known, and making them known was the major purpose of the overthrow they were planning. They knew that only riots made Johnny Q. Public think about conditions behind the walls, that only through violent protest would prison authorities make even the smallest commitment to better those conditions. Racial prejudices were set aside so there would be unanimity during the takeover, at least among the Chicanos and whites. Tension between both of those cliques and the blacks was too high for any sit-down discussions to be practical. Since there were less than 200 blacks among the 1,156 men in the prison, their advice and consent didn't seem important to the planning of the riot. But plenty of secret meetings were going on between the Aryan Brotherhood and the Mexican Mafia.

It was from a white bro I'd known during my last five years in the joint that I learned the details of the takeover. I knew his information was reliable because he was one of the lieutenants in the Aryan Brotherhood. First, though, I had to listen to his gripes.

"I don't know how long the brothers can maintain and keep cool," he told me, "because The Man is always fuckin' us over. If one of us has a good job, he moves him to another one. Some of the brothers have been tryin' to enter the educational department and take some courses, to try for once to show somethin' for the time they're doin', but the cocksucker always gives us some bullshit excuse about why he won't let us in. Last time, one of the bros was told he couldn't get in because there are too many female teachers! 'You guys are bikers and too dangerous for us to let loose with the women.' What the fuck does he think we're gonna do, eat the broads out in front of the goddamn screws?"

We both got a laugh out of that—it's been known to happen.

"That fuckass Deputy Warden Montoya, all you have to do to get on his wrong side is have a goddamned Harley Davidson tattoo. I swear, he hates bikers more than he hates whites. He dishes out more crap to us brothers—as if it wasn't bad enough in this cesspool without him layin' his power trips on us.

"The thing that's getting' to everyone, whites, niggers, Mexicans alike, is that this place is gettin' so fucking overcrowded there's almost no room to fart. Everywhere you turn, somebody's there. Their feet stink, there's about six inches between you and the dude in the bed next to you and you can't even move your arm over without hittin' someone in the face. Here's eighty-five guys crammed into a dorm built to hold fifty. Some cells have two dudes in them now, so there goes all hope of privacy—locked in there with some asshole you might feel like pissin' on. It's impossible to have any quiet, with radios tuned to every station in the state and turned up to full volume. You try to sleep or read or even jerk off to some fine fantasy, but you can't, and you can't get away 'cause there ain't no place to go, not one place in this whole friggin' joint where you can go to be alone so maybe you can snivel to yourself about how bad you feel instead of punchin' someone out to relieve it.

"And of course, there's always the fuckin' food. You know, just a week ago they served us rotten turkey, so help me God, green, smelly, rotten turkey. About four hundred guys got the shits, but The Man just shrugged it off like it was nothin'. Have you noticed the guards?"

I told him I had, that they hadn't changed much since I'd left six months ago.

"No, man, they're worse, and they get worse every shit-eatin' day. There's a slew of these new ones, and they're the worst motherfuckers I've ever seen, all in their early twenties. One's only eighteen, and none of them have any training, except in how to carry a chip on their shoulder and a bad attitude. Here's some eighteen-year-old punk thinks he's hot shit 'cause he's wearin' a uniform and carryin' a club, been on the job four months and he walks up to a forty-five-year-old lifer and orders him around like he's some dumb dog. The age difference alone is enough t'make the con resent the screw, let alone the way the sonofabitch talks down to him. I tell you, bro, we've had it—we're gonna put a stop to it. We had it all planned, then a snivellin' snitch squelched it. But we're gonna roll again, when the time's right."

My friend was a tattooed bonafide biker from California who believed in white power to the max. His white brothers came before anybody or anything; right or wrong, the covered their action. He was known by inmates and administration alike as one of the prison's hardcore troublemakers. He came in on a two-to-ten-year term for forgery but earned another two-to-ten for manslaughter when he took part in a penitentiary murder with two of his tight white brothers. He usually lived in Cellblock 5 with the other "incorrigibles" but in November they'd all been moved to E-2. Although the transfer had been made to turn 5 into a more secure unit with electronically locked doors, the move into a minimum security dormitory astounded a lot of the guards as much as it pleased the sixty troublemakers who'd been relocated. It was after this transfer that riot rumbles began, all emanating from E-2.

The original plan revolved around a show that the local university radio station, KUNM, was going to broadcast from the prison gymnasium the first Saturday in December. The inmates were to take the deejays hostage, along with the guards assigned to the area, and use the broadcasting facilities to communicate to KUNM's statewide audience what conditions were like in the penitentiary and what demands would have to be met before the hostages were freed. When the administration got word of the scheme from the informer, they advised the radio station of it and cancelled the show. The deejays who'd set up the event didn't let that stop them. They knew the prison administration didn't like the media meddling in their business. They trusted their inmate contact, who denied a riot plan and called the cancellation a cover-up of all the crap going on inside. The deejays and KUNM made a lot of noise about their right of access, until finally they got permission to do a broadcast from inside the penitentiary in April or May of 1980, the exact date to be chosen later. Some riot planners decided they'd bide their time until then, since the show offered them such good access to hostages and broadcasting facilities. But others were not so patient.

There was a faction of the Aryan Brotherhood, together with a few Chicanos, that had been talking about an escape since the middle of November, when Cellblock 5 was transferred to E-2. When the riot plot reached them and there seemed to be a chance to take over the prison, they'd put it off. Taking over the institution had been this group's first preference anyway, with a few variations on the theme. Their idea was to get fifty mostly white brothers into the gym along with twenty to forty blacks who they'd stab to death (you don't need a reason to hate in prison—rage is so abundant you just need a scapegoat to act out on). When the slaughter was over, they'd take the hospital and psychology unit, hold the guards hostage, and drink, swallow, or shoot up all the drugs they could find. However, this idea was cancelled because it was deemed too impractical, and the group went with an escape plan instead. When the prison takeover didn't happen, they decided to go for the escape.

Eleven inmates were in on the deal. On Saturday night, December 8, one of them took a smuggled hacksaw blade and cut through the steel grillwork in his cell window while another kept watch across the hall. The next night, after the big Sunday dinner, thirty residents of Cellhouse 2, where the escape was to be staged, congregated in the back of the mess hall to surround six of the men who were in on the escape but from other cellblocks, and walk them past the Cellhouse 2 guard. This wasn't difficult to do, since the officers rarely knew exactly who lived in which unit. All eleven inmates jammed into the six-by-nine-foot cell where the hole had been cut in the window. When they were sure the guard in the tower was asleep, they climbed out of the window, one by one.

They'd been watching this tower guard for weeks and knew that he regularly slept on the job. All convicts knew that tower duty was the shit shift, so boring that the screws made a practice of using the time to catch up on their sleep. This was the second escape in two years that was accomplished right under the nose of a sleeping tower guard. These eleven men made it across a brightly lit lawn and cut a hole in part of the perimeter fence that was directly in the shadow of the tower. The guard was fired when the escape was finally discovered. He was in his early twenties, had been at the institution for only a year and, like most of the new officers, had far too little training in the realities likely to be encountered in a maximum-security prison. No one else was minding the store, either. According to security regulations, the control center and all the guard towers are supposed to be in telephone communication with each other every half hour. If a tower guard didn't call in, the control center was supposed to phone him to be sure the dude was awake, a built-in precaution for the boring nature of tower duty. Both the cellhouse guard and the supervisor for the night were given thirty-day suspensions for not paying attention to their jobs, but these slaps on the hand didn't begin to touch the problems caused by the laxness of security in the joint. Things were definitely unraveling in New Mexico's penitentiary.

A year before the escape, a former California corrections official did a study of the institution for the American Justice Institute. In that study he called the prison "one of the most poorly administered"[2] he'd ever encountered. Still, a year later, nothing had been done to upgrade the management. The New Mexico Attorney General investigated conditions in the penitentiary after the December 9 escape and told the public in his report what every inmate in the prison knew: the penitentiary had "a history of instability and poor planning"; management was rampant with "factionalism, poor communication, and apathy"; one of the worst problems was "the volatile condition of overcrowding and misuse of dormitories for medium security prisoners...We cannot afford to wait for another major incident and hope again that our resources and planning will come together before the situation becomes critical." He concluded that by staffing the institution with guards who were recent high-school graduates with no training for prison work, the state's officials were "playing Russian roulette with the lives of inmates, staff, and the public."[3]

Like I said, only a riot turns the bureaucrat's head around. This report, issued less than a month before the Russian roulette broke out on February 2, made no impression on prison officials, at least none they acted on. In spite of these findings, in spite of warnings from informers that riot plans were still in the air and weapons were being stashed in Dormitory E-2, the administration did nothing to tighten security. They held a lot of meetings to discuss the information and once sent a team in to search E-2. Nothing was found, but plenty was there.

In fact, the institution was being run so sloppily that the riot instigators began to wonder if The Man was daring them to start something. The riot control grills separating each dormitory from the main corridor of the prison hadn't been locked for the past six months. Even though these gates were being renovated to allow their electronic operation from the control center, guards were still supposed to lock them manually every night. They weren't doing it, however. Later they'd tell investigators that it was "too cumbersome" to do so; and the administration would say they felt no urgency about getting the grills hooked up electronically, though they could have gotten the job done in a matter of days. In addition to these dormitory grills there were two riot control gates that separated the north and south sides of the penitentiary from the control center. These were supposed to be locked every day at 4:30 PM, after daily activities were finished, but they too were being left unlocked at night. These are not just after-the-fact findings. The riot leaders observed this carelessness while it was happening. When "shatterproof" glass was installed in the wrap-around windows of the control center, the uprising instigators considered it another mark in their favor. They saw weaknesses that the prison authorities and legislators who approved the glass obviously didn't. The 3/16-inch-thick one-way bulletproof pane replaced small windows with steel grillwork that had been found to inhibit monitoring by causing blind spots, areas that couldn't be seen from the control center. Betting the new glass could be broken easily, the riot leaders counted the destruction of it as one of their first attack priorities.

On January 6, less than a month before the riot, a relatively minor racial incident bloomed into a situation that fired a move to set the uprising in motion sooner than planned. A fight broke out in Cellhouse 2 between Ronnie Stout, a white bro, and a black professional boxer. The boxer whipped Stout's ass and gave him two purple eyes. This angered the white clique. Ronnie Stout was a heavy in the prison. He'd done a lot of time and was about to get out on parole. He also had a twin brother, Donnie, who'd done as much time and had just come back on a new twelve-to-sixty-year sentence for armed robbery. They'd always had an exceptional bond with each other, pulling robberies together and sometimes using their resemblance to trade-off punishments. The twins talked a lot about a psychic connection they thought they had with each other. "I'd know something was wrong with Donnie and I'd get up and go wherever he was, no one could stop me when I felt it," Ronnie described it.

Donnie heard about the fight, probably more from the grapevine than ESP, and he was ready to jump to Ronnie's aid. He got members of the Aryan Brotherhood to go down to Ronnie's cell the next morning to discuss what kind of payback they should lay on the black responsible for the beating, but Ronnie told them he didn't want any trouble. He'd made his parole and was due to get out at the end of the month. A fight on his behalf would only fuck up his chance for freedom. He convinced his brother and the white brothers to forget the whole incident, and a race war was averted.

Deputy Warden Robert Montoya, however, had gotten word of the fight and the powwow about retribution. That afternoon he had Donnie Stout and his fifteen henchmen, along with the black prizefighter, locked up in Cellblock 3, the segregation unit, on the charge that they were plotting a race riot. Prison rules and regulations state that no inmate under investigation of a charge is to be kept in lockup for more than five days. At the end of five days, he has to be found guilty or set free. The prison's intelligence officer, Eugene Morgan, turned in a report to Montoya that stated the fight between Stout and the black was personal rather than racial, that nothing further would happen once the men were released from segregation. But Montoya didn't release them. Regardless of the findings and prison policy, he kept the men in lockup for sixteen more days. If one of the inmates hadn't gotten a letter through to the ACLU, they might have been there longer. As it was, an attorney called the warden and warned him that it was release or the courts. Only then were the 17 convicts returned to population.

Because the Deputy Warden had been creating episodes like this for the past five years, he'd become the most hated administrator in the institution. This incident was the last saddlebag. The riot leaders conferred and resolved that they'd move at the first opportunity. They thought they'd pick a Monday because there'd be more civilians in the offices to take as hostages, but they weren't setting any dates. They'd play it by ear, and everyone would have to be ready in a moment's notice. From then on, the instigators in E-2 spent their free time psyching themselves up for war.

I lay on my upper bunk that last night in January, somewhere between crying and pounding on the wall. The board members had granted me parole, but some sadistic twist in their natures made them choose April 23 as my release date. I knew I was going to get stuck in this riot. My friends weren't about to hold back for two weeks no less two months. I had no taste for an uprising. I just wanted to get out of the place and never see it again. I didn't want anything messing up my chance to do just that. But I was between a rock and a hard spot. If I got involved and vented my payback feelings, The Man would revoke my parole and send me up on new charges. If I didn't participate in the festivities, I could get my throat cut. I'd been in the joint long enough to know that you're either with a convict or against him and the choice means life or death, there's no middle ground. Yet the middle ground was exactly what I was going to have to find. The more I thought about it, the more depressed I got. Why in hell had the parole board made me wait? The question kept running through my head all night, even though I knew the answer as well as my name: they just don't give a damn about the lives they have such control over, they don't think of convicts as human beings, they think of us as animals. And by God, don't we become animals. By the time daybreak came I'd imagined myself smashing in the heads of every parole person who'd put me in this position.

# 3

*One cannot endure a penalty so monstrous as the lack of freedom without demanding of one's mind and body a labor at once delicate and brutal, a labor capable of warping the prisoner in a direction which takes him ever farther from the social world.*

—Jean Genet[1]

## 2:00 A.M., Saturday, February 2, 1980.

I was sitting on my bed talking to the guy in the next bunk when we were interrupted by the sound of yelling and screaming. My first thought was that The Man was taking some out-of-line inmates to lockup. Cellblock 3, the segregation unit, was just down the hall from me. It was a daily occurrence for a guard to be dragging a troublemaker through the corridor past my dorm, and equally as common for the screw to be smacking the con in the ribs with his stick all the way, but these cries were stronger than they usually were, and got my curiosity up. I jumped down from my bunk and walked into the shower room to check it out through a window that overlooked the control center and main corridor. I saw screaming inmates all right, seventy-five to a hundred of them, running from the south end up to the control center booth, waving all kinds of makeshift weapons. Those in the front of this mob were dragging a barely crawling, naked, blindfolded screw by a belt looped around his neck. Those behind were kicking him in the ribs and butt and whacking him in the legs, which, like his arms, were tied. I saw someone bring a chain down hard across his back and the man crumbled; but the crowd was determined to keep him moving. They kicked him more viciously in the ass, whipping him with their pipes while the one holding the "leash" yanked it hard, until finally the hostage got back on his hands and knees and resumed his painful crawl.

"Unlock the gate or we'll beat the shit out of your friend here," the rioter holding the belt demanded of the guard inside the booth, who couldn't be seen through the new mirrored window.

Just minutes earlier, that booth guard, Officer Lawrence Lucero, had ordered the guards on the north side to lock the north grill. He'd heard one of the riot leaders announce, over a confiscated two-way radio, that they'd taken over the prison, were holding seven guards hostage and wanted a meeting with the Governor, the news media and the Deputy Secretary of Corrections. Lucero had imme-

17

diately phoned the chief of security, Emanuel Koroneos, at his home to advise him that a riot was in progress. Louis C. de Baca, one of the guards on foot patrol outside the building, had also heard on his radio the rioter's demands and ran into the penitentiary to help his co-workers. He remembered that renovations in progress on the electronic systems would make it difficult for Lucero to get out of the control booth on his own. Because the door wasn't operating electrically, the only way it could be opened from the inside was by reaching through the bars of the door, with key in hand, and blindly attempting to fit it into the lock. If Officer C. de Baca hadn't been on the ball, the guard inside the booth would have been cursing the inefficiency of the administration as he perched there, locked into a sitting duck position, while all hell broke loose around him; if indeed he stayed alive that long. As it was, Officer C. de Baca made it to the control center, pushing through the mob of rioters who were shouting demands for the grill to be opened.

"Unlock the gate, motherfucker, or you're gonna have one dead screw on your hands," the lead rioter yelled, tugging on his hostage's "leash."

"No way," Officer Lucero replied from inside.

He didn't have the ability to open the north grill anyway, since it wasn't electronically connected to the control panel. In refusing the rioters' demand, Lucero was following the officers' code: don't give in to threats by inmates. He had to bear the consequences of heeding that code by watching the rioters attack their naked hostage, a twenty-five year old guard who'd worked at the penitentiary for only a year. They beat him with pipes, metal table legs, chains, and homemade knives until they drew blood. Then they stopped to see if Lucero had changed his mind about opening the gate, but he hadn't, and the convicts again surged around their kneeling victim, kicking, punching, pounding him with their weapons until he fell unconscious. Maybe they let up then because he looked dead. Officer Lucero would later say he thought they'd killed him.

"See what you've done now?" someone yelled at Lucero. "If you don't open up, it's gonna be you next, suckface."

But the officer wouldn't give in. While a small group dragged the unconscious guard's body back to the south end, the bulk of the rioters started beating on the control center's new shatterproof window with their pipes. A mop bucket was hurled at it several times, then someone grabbed a fire extinguisher off the wall and hurled it against the glass. On the third throw, the safety window began cracking. Shatterproof my ass! As slivers of glass began splintering inside the control booth, Officer C. de Baca unlocked the booth and he and Officer Lucero ran out. They must have panicked, because they didn't attempt to stop the rioters by flooding the place with the tear gas stored in the booth for just such emergencies. Nor did they think to take the keys to the rest of the institution, hanging in plain sight on the keyboard. Lucero, twenty-four years old with three years experience in the penitentiary, and C. de Baca, twenty-two, with only one year, ran out of the prison's front entrance into the safety of the main tower. They were the first officers to escape the riot.

Five minutes after the rioters began their attack on the control booth, the newly installed bulletproof glass had a gaping hole in it and the inmates were in command of the nerve center of the institution, with access to practically every unit. Seven or eight of them pulled the glass loose and stepped through the open window into the booth. They demolished everything in sight, then opened the trap door that led to the compartment where all the riot gear was kept and handed it out: teargas guns, bombs, batons, riot helmets, gas masks. It was a bizarre scene, like some celebration of D-Day in a POW camp. As the weapons came up, the crowd grabbed them, waving them in the air, putting on the gas masks and helmets. Someone accidentally fired one of the teargas guns, and the corridor filled with asphyxiating smoke and fumes. The mob broke into fits of choking and gasping, but those fits didn't drain the rioters of excitement. They were wild with their newfound power, jumping up and down in raging jigs. It was bedlam. The shouting became a roaring wave of war cries and curses.

"Let's go get the snitches!"

"Burn the fuckin' records, man, let's go!"

"Let's hit the pharmacy and find us some reds!"

Inside the control booth, a Chicano rioter was unrolling the folded American flag put there every night for safekeeping. "Hey man, don't you think this would make a fine poncho?" Answering himself, he took a pair of scissors, cut a hole in the middle of the flag and slipped it over his head. Later he would become one of the main negotiators, talking over the two-way radio and wearing his American flag poncho until it got too bloody to be comfortable.

The original seventy-five rioters who'd stormed the control center increased in number as the other freed inmates from the south side joined them. A large group invaded the administration offices behind the control booth and began tearing them apart, going through desks and filing cabinets, throwing everything inside them into piles in the middle of each office's floor and setting them on fire, burning every record of every convict in the penitentiary. They went through the I.D. office in the basement, where the private property, including money, of newly arrived inmates was kept. Some lucky dude found approximately $1200 in there, money that was never recorded and is probably still floating around the penitentiary's underground stashes; unless some con has already spread it around the joint by purchasing smack, grass, LSD, or covering gambling debts.

The reveling and rioting inmates now had free access to phones, and used it to call wives, cousins and friends. People in Canada and New York knew there was a riot going on in New Mexico before downtown Santa Fe, eleven miles away, knew about it. Their friends cheered them on, told them: "More power to you." These were words they would have to regret, as I did, when the power turned barbaric. But at this early point in the uprising, just about every inmate in the prison, myself included, was silently congratulating the rioters for pulling it off. Some of the snitches in Cellblock 4 probably were, too. The freeing of bonds is always exhilarating, at least in the beginning.

While one group was assaulting the control center and the administrative offices, totally demolishing everything in sight, another had opened the north grill and was running through the main north side corridor shouting: "This is a riot, let's go!" They opened Cellblock 6 and the old men's dormitory where I was, but when the leaders went to get their friends out of Cellblock 3, segregation, they found they hadn't taken the right keys. A few went back to get them from the control center, but more stayed. They were getting near the snitch cage and they smelled blood. Some of them stormed up the grill that separated that cage, Cellblock 4, from the corridor, and taunted the snitches with threats:

"Breathe your last breaths, motherfuckers...."

"Cause you ain't got long to live..."

"Just as long as it takes to get the keys, you sniveling cunts..."

"You're gonna pay, long and hard, can you see it now, suckface?"

But for the moment, luck was with the snitches. The rioters weren't able to find the keys to Cellblock 4, and its electronic operation, though working, was jammed. The snitches would have plenty of time to barricade their cells, though they didn't know it. For them, the next few hours were ones of grim expectation.

There were fifteen guards on duty inside the prison, less than half, it was later determined, than the number working at other similarly overcrowded prisons across the nation; this in spite of the fact that the Penitentiary of New Mexico was known to be primed for an imminent explosion. Seven of these guards, including the shift commander Captain Roybal, had been taken hostage on the south side. One was being hidden by sympathetic inmates in Dormitory F-1. Another, Officer Mike Hernandez, assigned to Dormitory D-1, had locked himself into the educational unit, which, along with D-1, was closed off from the rest of the institution by a corridor grill. Officer Lucero, on duty in the control center, had run out of the prison. This left five more officers, all of them on the north end of the building, for the inmates to deal with, along with one civilian, the hospital technician.

When the rioters gained access to the control center, these six staff members began to seek safety from the mob they knew would soon break through the north security grill. The officer assigned to Cellhouse 6, Antonio Vigil, who'd worked at the penitentiary for twenty-two years, and Valentin Martinez, a ten-year veteran assigned this night to the snitches' Cellblock 4, phoned the guard on duty outside in Tower 3 and informed him that they would be hiding in the basement crawl space near the gas chamber. They warned him not to transmit their hiding place over the two-way radios because the inmates were also using the two-ways and would pick up the information. They chose a good spot, and remained hidden and unharmed for the duration of the uprising. The infirmary technician, Ross Maez, another old-timer, with twenty-two years at the prison, locked himself, along with seven inmate patients, in a small room at the far end of the upstairs section of the hospital. The last three guards, Officers Larry Mendoza, Edward Ortega, and Ramon Gutierrez, all assigned to Cellblock 3 where the hardcore troublemakers were kept in segregation, locked themselves in the basement area of the cellblock. Mendoza and Guiterrez were both young. One had been a guard for three years, the other for only one. Ortega, on the other hand, was a twenty-three year veteran of the institution. Nevertheless, it was Mendoza who proved to be the more alert officer this night. Realizing he had left the main key to Cellblock 3 in a small box in the vestibule of the middle level, he crawled upstairs and retrieved it. While he was there, the rioters who had just realized they couldn't open the grill saw him and yelled: "Open the gate, Mendoza, or when we do get it open you're dead." But Mendoza refused and returned to the basement, locking himself and the other two officers in an area used to store bedding.

By now about thirty inmates had entered the hospital unit. They went straight for the pharmacy and the filing cabinet where they knew all the drugs were kept. They set about prying the cabinet open and in minutes had themselves a candy store of every kind of downer you can think of, from valium to Miltown to reds to codeine, even liquid Demerol, available to all comers in any dosage desired. There were also hypodermic needles and syringes for those who liked a more potent hit. The state had a purchasing policy that required them to buy in bulk, a policy that came in handy for the rioters, or so they thought as they stood there shooting up, swallowing pills, indulging in far more than their systems would eventually be able to handle. They filled up shoeboxes with colorful capsules and tablets, along with bottles of Demerol, syringes and needles, heaped pills into their pockets, and staggered euphorically back into the hallway to turn-on their friends. They never bothered to look in the upstairs hospital, so the health technician and his seven inmate patients weren't seen, and in fact remained hidden for the duration of the riot. Nor did the rioters lay the unit to waste as they had every other place they'd entered. Their only interest in the infirmary was drugs. Once they had them, they unconsciously paid homage to their benefactor.

While these thirty were raiding their candy store, another group was tearing apart the psychological unit. One thing the rioters seemed set on was burning every record in the prison. They dumped all the files into the middle of the floor, along with carpets, wooden chairs and tables, and set fire to them. This was going to be a big blaze, not like the smaller ones in the administrative offices. They were out to thoroughly destroy the unit.

"Hey you guys, we're burnin' down that fucker Orner's headquarters, let the bastard see how we feel about him, "they warned those of us in the old men's dorm, which was just above the psych unit. "You're gonna suffocate to death if you don't split. We know lots of you dudes are too old to join with us, some of you got short time before you'll be gettin' home, so maybe you don't want any part of all this shit and just want to sit it out in here. We can dig it, but it looks like you're bein' forced into it regardless. Either that or die from the smoke."

I sympathized with their wanting to get back at the head of the psych unit, Dr. Marc Orner. He was a longtime member of the current twenty-year old administration and an abuser of the snitch system, a system that had landed just about every con with any balls at all in the Hole at least once. None of us felt like leaving the dormitory though, in spite of the smoke that began to drift up. Between the haze it created and the crazed way these guys appeared, it was like standing at the entrance to hell. Half of them looked like space soldiers, with their gas masks and teargas guns, the other half looked like old west outlaws, bandanas pulled up over their faces, wielding pipes and batons like they were rifles. Through this entrance to hell came a few bare-faced rioters passing around the pill-filled shoeboxes. I refused the offer, but others in the dorm took handfuls, hoping a high would make the craziness easier to handle. I wanted to keep my head straight and clear so I'd get through it all in one piece, because this was clearly going to be worse than I'd ever imagined. I'd been watching dudes line up in the corridor just a few minutes before, about twenty of them, queuing up like it was a shooting gallery, waiting their turn to push some Demerol into their veins, then staggering out into the crowd waving their pipes and table legs in the air, whooping and hollering about "killing that asshole that burned me…" Whatever exhilaration I'd felt earlier was gone. As for getting out and walking among these madmen or staying in the dorm and taking our chances with the smoke, we were of one mind: we opted for the smoke.

"Okay, that's your problem then, don't say we didn't warn you," the gasmasked spokesman for the group told us, and walked away with his platoon.

They could have slit our throats there and then for not wanting to join them, but these cons seemed to understand our stake in not getting involved. We doubted that others would as the riot progressed.

# 4

*If you are a free person that's a racist, if you hate, this is one of the few places where you can come and exercise it with encouragement and impunity. The emphasis of this institution is man's inhumanity against man, and to oppress an inmate at any cost. There's a penalty here for being respectable to an inmate.*

—INMATE, STATEVILLE PRISON, Joliet, Illinois [1]

Prison is a jungle where the strong survive, and only the strong. It's not so different from life in that respect, except that a penitentiary is a zoo and the inmates are caged animals. They're fed like animals, treated like animals, and encouraged to behave like animals toward one and other. The meals are slopped on metal plates just like they are for animals in a zoo. The food itself, basically starch and pork, is geared to keep a human functioning on the dullest animal level. There is nothing in the prison to help a man remember that he is a human being who can evolve out of his past mistakes. Everything points to his failure and hammers it into his consciousness. Respect is quickly forgotten; none is shown to convicts by any prison administrator or guard, except the respect won by being the toughest animal and causing the greatest fear. I once heard a politician say that the law of survival meant that if you're going to survive you must be king. In the joint, if you have any intentions of surviving, you've got to be the king animal. How you relate to people here is completely different from how you're used to relating on the outside. You can't be nice; nice guys don't last. You quickly find out that kindness is a weakness in the joint. If you tell a guy, "Yeah, I'll loan you a dollar," he'll think: 'Look at this weak sonofabitch, he's easy, I'll hit him for fifty dollars next time.' Or he'll come back every week for that same dollar or that same candy bar you first offered. It's one big head game that breaks down to the golden rule of survival in the convict jungle: do unto others before they do it to you.

I first arrived at the Penitentiary of New Mexico on a ten-to-fifty year armed robbery conviction in 1962, twenty-two years old and scared shitless. I'd been prepared for the hard facts of prison life by some parole violators in the county jail who were there while I was waiting to be sentenced. They told me that if I was going to make it, I'd have to stand up for myself the first time something came down. And plenty, they said, would come down. The majority of the population at the time was Chicano, some 600 of them, with about 200 blacks and

24

only 100 whites. For the first time in my life I was going to be part of a minority group, an even more vulnerable position in a prison than it is in the outside world. They warned me that when young white guys came into population at Santa Fe (which we called the penitentiary because of its proximity to that city), they'd get hit on for a piece of ass. The new white boy had a choice: stand up for himself or get pushed to the limit for the rest of his time there. My first month was spent in Quarantine, where all newcomers are kept for thirty day while they're given a battery of physical, mental, and emotional tests before joining the rest of the prison population. Why all this is done I've never understood. The administration certainly never used the results to help rehabilitate anyone, and many men with psychological problems were sent to coexist with the general prison population. Nevertheless, a week after I'd been released from Quarantine, I had a chance to prove what kind of convict I was going to be.

I'd been assigned to a dormitory, a dangerous place for a novice to the prison game. A convict didn't get a cell of his own until he'd done some time and proven he wasn't a troublemaker. Once he earned it, he'd be given a cellhouse unit and a "house." He'd be free to move in population for meals and work, but at night he'd have the luxury of a locked cell where nobody could attack him. Then the sound of the metal door snapping shut would be a welcome one. But in the dormitories, when that door clanked every night at lockup, it was time to be on guard. For the first few months that sound sent chills up my spine, but eventually I got used to it. In prison you adjust to closing metal doors or you go crazy. In prison, you adjust to every kind of inhumanity or you go berserk. I was sitting on my bunk one Saturday afternoon when a black convict walked up to me.

"Hey, how about helpin' us out?" he said.

I asked him what he meant.

"Well, we've been checkin' you out, and me and a couple buddies decided we wanna fuck your butt. All the white guys that come in here, they all turn around and help out the brothers, and the brothers go ahead and take care of them. We'll take care of you, too. We won't let the Mexicans fuck with you."

I told him I wasn't at all interested.

"Well, if you don't, we'll just come over tonight and take it anyway, so you just think about how you want it."

I was a fairly naïve twenty-two year old and had never been approached by a man sexually. I also held the racial prejudices that were as normal among white folks in 1962 as apple pie and mom were, so the prospect that stared me in the face was triply offensive. Fortunately I'd made the acquaintance of an old-timer in another unit, and I went to him with my problem. He listened and was typically noncommittal.

"Well, what do you want to do about it?" he asked me.

I told him I only knew I didn't want anything to do with the dude and asked what he thought I *should* do about it.

"If you don't stand up to them now, they're gonna go ahead and fuck you and you're gonna end up a jailhouse punk. You'll have a hard way to go that way. I seen a lot of white boys get fucked by the blacks and the Chicanos in the five years I been here. Most of them were raped and they all became punks, jailhouse ladies. If you stand up to them, you might get your ass whipped, but when it's all over, they won't bother you no more."

I explained that standing up to them was what I had in mind, but the guy that approached me was big, plus he had friends. How was I going to fight them all and come out alive?

"I got somethin' that'll help you," he told me, stomping out the butt of his Camel. He left his bunk and went into the shower room. When he came back, he handed me a two-foot piece of radiator pipe, which I quickly put down my trousers, holding it against my thigh with one hand. He hadn't sawed off the pipe in that quick trip, he just kept his personal arsenal of weapons stashed somewhere in the lavatory. It was for just such battles that these weapon stashes were kept by most of the hardcore cons.

That night I lay on top of my bunk, waiting, the pipe by my side. At about 1:30 in the morning, I saw my would-be attacker walking up the aisle toward me. I tensed and took a deep breath.

He reached my bed and whispered: "Hey, you ready, boy?"

I told him yeah, I was ready.

"Okay," he said in a satisfied low voice. "Let's go to the dayroom, we got something for you you're gonna love."

I got up and he started walking in front of me. I thought to myself, I got something for you too, sucker. He didn't quite get to turn around before I slammed the pipe against the side of his head. He didn't go down, just stood there like he was in shock, his eyes wide, staring at me as if he couldn't understand how this could happen to him. I hit him again, this time across the collarbone. He let out a short yell and fell over backwards. I let him lay there and went toward the dayroom for his buddies. There was only one, and he was standing in the doorway, alerted by his friend's yell.

"What's happenin', where's brother Jones?" he asked, apparently not seeing the pipe in my hand.

"Brother Jones isn't comin' tonight," I answered, and swung the pipe into his face. He wailed in pain, then started yelling for help. He got it. The lights went on and four guards raced into the dormitory. My two victims had to go to the hospital, but not before the last one I hit told The Man that I'd attacked them for no apparent reason. I gave my side of the story, but I was still thrown in the maximum detention unit, the "Hole." I guess they figured the two blacks had gotten punishment enough from my beating, because I was the only one who got sent there. My crash course in prison survival had begun. It was a survival that required I develop the emotional, mental and physical sensitivity of an armored combat tank.

The Hole is located in the basement under Cellblock 3, the lockup unit for troublemakers, and just behind Death Row. I always thought that was ironic. Like waiting on Death Row for that long, legally delayed date with cyanide, being in the Hole could make a man wish he were dead. There are ten Holes, six-by-nine-foot cells with no window, no ventilation, no lights, just darkness. Two of the ten Holes are padded for the more violent resister. Most off the time you're stripped and thrown in naked, as I was. All you're allowed is a thin blanket, a toothbrush and a metal cup. A mattress is given to you at ten at night and taken away at six in the morning. They feed you one meal every three days and six slices of white bread for the two days in between. There's a faucet in the cell, but there's water in it only when the guard comes and turns it on from outside. He does that three times a day—morning, noon and evening. You've got nothing to store the water in so you've got to drink what you can, wash up, and fill your cup so you've got some to last till the next time it's turned on. It's a thirsty stretch from 6:00 PM to 6:00 AM with one cup of water. The toilet is a hole in the floor that you squat over. It flushes from the outside. The guards think it's funny not to flush it for a few days in a row, playing their little mind games with you, asking every time they come by: "Does it smell pretty good in there?" When it's hot, like it was when I went in that first time, it got to stinking pretty bad. There isn't any toilet paper either, so even if they kept the thing flushed, after a few days you get to smelling pretty rank yourself. In the winter it's freezing cold so you don't have to worry about the odor; you have enough to do trying to keep warm with one thin blanket and no heat. The only time I saw light was when The Man opened the door to give me the mattress or meals. Though I couldn't communicate via visits or letters with anyone from the outside world, I could carry on a conversation with the even more unfortunate dudes on Death Row, or with those who'd been thrown in other Holes, by yelling though the vent and listening to what they shouted back through their vent. That is, unless someone was screaming to get out or throwing a fit. After three days, I didn't have the energy to carry on much small talk. My thoughts began to give way to fantasies about food. All kinds of food. I'd turn those slices of white bread into pound cake and eat them slowly, chewing each bite until it was liquid, savoring the delicious meal I was making of it in my mind. Years later I heard a story about an Armenian woman who was being marched and starved out of her land by the Turkish army. She stayed alive by eating one pomegranate seed a day and imagining it to be a juicy slice of lamb. It was like that for me.

At last my ten days were up and I saw light again, at first painful for my unaccustomed eyes. But I wasn't released back into population. The rule was that after a stint in the Hole a convict was sent upstairs to Segregation, Cellblock 3. Compared to my recent dungeon life, Cellblock 3 seemed like the Waldorf, at least for the first day. There was plenty of light now, but in such an ugly, disintegrating place it seemed a cruelty. I wasn't allowed any distractions either: No reading material, no little luxury items from the canteen that make prison life bearable, like cigarettes, candy bars and Kool-Aid. I was still locked up all day and all night in a six-by-nine cell, though with clothing and a bed this time, as well as a toilet that flushed and toilet paper. But there was no exercise, no fresh air. There was more food, hardly edible as it was. It was served on paper plates and 99 percent of the time it was cold because of the long trek from the kitchen to the cellblock. The major diversions were shower time—three times a week we got to walk the catwalk to the shower, stand under the running water for five minutes, and walk back to our cells—and the weekly one-hour session called exercise time, when we'd be let out of our cells one at a time to walk up and down the corridor and shoot the breeze with other inmates on the same tier. Radios weren't allowed, and there was no TV. Three or four days out of seven some con would entertain us all by stuffing a towel in his toilet and flooding the hallway with three or four inches of water. Since we weren't allowed out of our cells, the guards would have to clean it up while we got laughs out of watching them take off their shoes, roll up their pants and mop away, cussing all the time. Aside from that, the only recreation available was writing endless numbers of letters, or beating off three times a day to an imaginary lover. Sometimes the noise level would prevent either of these diversions. Inmates would start yelling at each other, or at the guards, or banging on the bars, just for something to break the monotony. Idle time is rampant throughout the prison population, but in lockup and in the Hole there's nothing *but* idle time. And then there were the mind games the guards pulled: holding back the mail and taunting the convict with it, denying visiting privileges when the visitor was waiting downstairs after traveling fifty miles to spend her monthly hour talking with her son or lover or husband or brother. Every day in lockup an inmate got fed a little more hate.

After two weeks in Cellblock 3, the captain called me down to his office and told me he was going to put me back into population. If I hurt anyone else, he told me, I'd be locked up again. I was released from Segregation that day and assigned to another dormitory, right below the first one I'd been in. The word had traveled. When I walked in, two black guys came up to me.

"Listen, man, we heard what happened upstairs. Don't worry about that happenin' here, we don't want no shit to come down," they assured me.

I was given a lot of respect from that day on. I learned how to survive and got thick-skinned and tougher than I'd ever been in the days when I was committing the robberies that put me in the joint. That's why I ended up spending nine years in the joint before I got paroled. I became a member of the white clique, which at the time hadn't turned into anything as serious as the Aryan Brotherhood. It was just a matter of power in numbers, and since there were so few of us in the pen, we let solidarity be our strength. I had plenty of bad examples to follow—bad in terms of the prissy image most of society has for the way a convict *should* learn to behave, but good for hardening me to the rude facts of prison existence.

The administration itself fostered the hardcore education of inmates by throwing newcomers, with only one-to-five year sentences, in with someone who had a lot of time: Fifty, a hundred years, maybe life. The lifer isn't any too pleased to be looking at a guy better off than he is, who's getting out in maybe six months, so there's tension between them. With so much idle time on their hands, that tension grows in their minds and soon they're at each other's throats. All of a sudden this newcomer, who may have come in just wanting to do his time peacefully and get out, is staring at another six months tagged onto his sentence because the older con riled him and The Man labeled the "fish"—our name for new inmates—a troublemaker. The administration, after all, has to be in there with the lifer a lot longer than with the guy who's only doing one-to-five, so the lifer gets the consideration. The Man may play sadistic games with the convicts, but he's also got his sly way of giving in to the power they wield. He doesn't want any outbreaks of rebellion that might catch the public's attention.

This is another example to add to the long list of how little the prison officials care about *rehabilitating* the inmates. When I came in, there were honor units for the dudes who'd been there a long time and were doing their stints peacefully. The administrators could have encouraged these old-timers to get together with the new arrivals and wise them up to what they were up against in population:

tell them how borrowing money or getting into any kind of debt could lead to their being beaten, stabbed or becoming someone's "kid"—a jailhouse punk who runs errands, cleans house, gets butt-fucked or gives a blow job whenever his "owner" wants; or how hardcore cons put pressure on the families of the dudes who owe them money, writing to a friend on the street that so-and-so owes them, which sends the friend to the guy's wife or relatives saying "You gotta pay up on his debt or we're gonna beat his ass in the joint." These peaceful old-timers could have offered help to the newcomers in case any of these things came to pass, but they didn't and the administration didn't encourage them to either. Nothing but survival of the strongest was encouraged in the Penitentiary.

It took six years for my hardcore training to throw me into a role I never expected to be in—that of a killer. I was head cook in the kitchen then. One Friday morning a fish came in from Quarantine to work on the cleanup detail. He was a young, tall, muscular man fresh out of Viet Nam who insisted on being called Eagle Beak and throwing his weight around to prove what a bad-ass dude he was. He zeroed in on one of my regular Chicano helpers, hassling him all morning with racial innuendos that quickly turned into blatant obscenities and name-calling. My sidekick was handling his end of the abuses just fine so I didn't step in, figuring the fish would talk himself out. But he got physical about it and pushed the Chicano against the wall.

"Hey, leave the kid alone," I yelled over to him.

Eagle Beak let go like he was holding a hot coal and came up to me. "Okay, I'll let him alone," he said, then smacked me hard in the jaw with his fist.

Common sense won over my instant reflex to kick the shit out of him. Aside from the fact that he was too large for me to successfully fight with my bare hands, I didn't want to get into it with him right there in the kitchen. I'd worked myself up into a good job—not easy to come by in prison—and I didn't want to blow it over some fish trying to prove he had balls. "Man, that hurt, I wish you wouldn't do that any more," I told him with ominous warning in my voice. He got the message and didn't cause any more trouble for the rest of the day.

The next morning was another matter, though. I was chopping lettuce for the Sunday salad when Eagle Beak walked up threateningly close and said calmly: "I was thinkin' about what happened yesterday. I figure that the job I did on you wasn't good enough. Let's me and you get down and get it right this time."

I kept on chopping and answered: "Man, I don't want to fight you."

But he popped me again, this time with such force he made my nose bleed. He laughed when he saw the blood and started coming at me again, but the carving knife I was holding reached his belly first. It was a long, French chef's knife I'd just sharpened that morning and it pierced him clear through. He groaned and clutched his stomach and, after a few moments of staggering, crumpled to the floor. Someone had to go get the guard; he hadn't been around to hear the fight. Eagle Beak was taken to the hospital and I was sent to lockup while the administration investigated the event.

Eagle Beak died ten days later. After two weeks in Segregation I was called into the warden's office. To my amazement he told me they weren't going to press murder charge against me. Why? Because the District Attorney didn't have a murder weapon. It seems the knife with which I'd killed Eagle Beak was the sharpest one in the kitchen, so the unthinking prison employee who was chief steward cleaned it off and went right on using it. When the D.A. came to the penitentiary to gather his evidence against me, he went to the kitchen and just about blew a fuse when he saw the steward using it to cut a roast. Without the knife, there wasn't a case. I'd gotten tight enough with my co-workers that they didn't go for The Man's promises of reward if they'd come up with a story that would earn a conviction. They just told the truth: It was self-defense, started by the victim.

The warden closed our interview by saying, "Well the guy is dead, he had no friends here, and I know he was pickin' on you. Do you think you can go back to population and behave yourself?"

Naturally, I answered yes.

I didn't get convicted for the killing, but I did pay the prison price. It was on my record. The parole board deny my release for three more years. At that point, I didn't care. I was young and carried an I-don't-give-a-fuck attitude about everything except my own safety and sanity, which were by then well protected. I belonged to a strong clique, and after my bout with Eagle Beak everyone, including myself, thought I was a hot-shit, bad-ass, hardcore motherfucker that nobody better mess with. The administration thought so too, and instead of sending me back to a dormitory or cellhouse in regular population, assigned me to the maximum security Cellblock 5, the toughest unit in the penitentiary.

There I got a post-graduate education in how to be the baddest bully in the joint. My teachers were the most incorrigible troublemakers there; some were, at least to my mind, criminally insane. These men got their rocks off harassing other inmates so they could watch them snivel in fear. They never fought or fucked with each other, but they made it their goal to bulldog the rest of the prison population. In fact, they ran the place, even the administration was afraid of them. The top echelon of the Chicano and white cliques lived in Southside Cellblock 5.

A black in the cellblock was unheard of, he wouldn't have lasted an hour. Even a white or Chicano couldn't move in without being "co-signed" by at least two other Cellblock 5 cons; that is, if he valued his life. No one ever tried voluntarily to bust the party, but if they had, they'd be faced with thirty men, every one of them wielding a weapon of some sort, whether a pipe, straight razor, shop-made knife, or Molotov cocktail. My toughen-up teachers had plenty of time on their hands to think about ways of getting and stashing their arsenals, and devised some cunning hiding places and smuggling schemes. The administration and guards knew all of this was happening and would regularly shake down the dorms and cellblocks. (It wasn't just the hardcore cellblock inmates who stashed weapons, though they were the best-armed men in the prison.) But for every weapon discovered, there were two to take its place. The convicts took their stash of weapons seriously, it was their main power, and often it had saved a dude's ass or life in a fight, as the pipe had for me when I first arrived in the prison. The Man looked the other way for the most part, as long as these arsenals were being used by inmates against other inmates. It's only when rumors of a riot came down that the administration made a real effort to find them.

All things considered, the inmates of Cellblock 5 were left alone to work over whomever they wanted as long as they didn't get in The Man's way. In fact, the administration used Cellblock 5 to do a lot of their dirty work for them. One "house" in the cellblock was always left free so that a new arrival, a fish who'd been giving the guards a hard time, could be thrown in there for a day, sometimes two, to scare him. And it would scare the poor bastard all right. The kid would catch hell, get beaten, kicked, raped, yelled at and robbed. He'd come out of that cell in a state of shock, wondering what he did to deserve being thrown in with such a bunch of maniacs. I've seen them dribbling at the mouth with eyes rolled up in their heads when The Man finally came and took them away. I remember one kid who'd just been transferred from Arizona. He thought he was a big shot, so the guards threw him in the empty cell. As soon as The Man left, someone got out his pipe and started in on the kid, hitting him with it all the way down the catwalk to the cellblock doorway. He was taken out then and there and spent a considerable time in the infirmary. The beating struck so much fear in him that he asked to do the rest of his time locked up in the protection unit, which he did. Anyone who asked for lockup in protection got it, but he'd have to sign a waiver releasing the penitentiary from any responsibility for what happened to him if he ever wanted to get back into population. This kid didn't pick an easy solution. Protection is also a twenty-four hour lockup, no-exercise stint that shot a man's reputation to hell. Anyone who chose not to stand up and fight, but to hide instead in the protection unit with the snitches and baby rapers, was despised. He was considered weak, the one thing survivors never allowed themselves to be.

Besides taking care of the administration's troublemakers, the men of Cellblock 5 specialized in personal paybacks. Anyone who burned them or their friends was in for disaster. In the joint, where there's little else to think about, old grudges grow to vendetta proportions. One day, a Cellblock 5 resident I'll call Barnes got word that an old buddy who'd burned him on the streets for $300 worth of dope had just come out of Quarantine and into population. Barnes got two friends to lure the dude up to the cellblock, where only someone new in the joint would dare to go. As they were bringing him up, inmates in Quarantine, which at that time was in Cellblock 4, just across the hall from 5, started warning him not to go in there, but it was too late: Barnes and ten of his close bros were standing in the middle of the catwalk, waiting. The welcher was pushed toward them then dragged into a cell where the eleven men did a job on him. He kept yelling for help but it didn't do him any good. Only one guard was on duty, and he stood at the cellblock entrance asking what was going on. He knew very well what was happening, but he was too chickenshit to come in. Instead, he headed to the office phone to call for assistance. He was stopped by four Chicanos who'd been stationed to watch for just such a possibility. They got to him just as he was about to dial. Surrounding but not touching him they warned: "Man, you better get the fuck off the phone and disappear for a while or we're gonna get you on the floor, too."

The officer knew they meant it and split. He couldn't have done anything for the welcher anyway. By then the poor guy was nearly beaten to death. His teeth were knocked out, both eyes were blackened, and his nose was broken and bloody. When they were finished working him over, Barnes and his ten buddies dragged the unconscious welcher across the hall and dumped him back in Cellblock 4, Quarantine. All thirty residents of Cellblock 5 followed, myself included, walking into Quarantine as if we lived there. It was payback time for warning the welcher. A few noses were busted and eyes darkened before Barnes stopped the action to ask: "Okay, any of you friends of this guy, any of you want to speak up for him?" There was silence. Though there were seventy of them and only thirty of us, we'd completely subdued them. Barnes decided that while he was there he might as well take a little treasure. Shaking a pillow out of its case, he announced: "Okay, every one of you sons of bitches, throw your canteen into this sack." Each of us grabbed ourselves a pillowcase and got into the act, walking up and down the catwalk in partners, going into each cell and strong-arming everyone in Quarantine for their precious stashes and valuables; everyone except the four or five old-timers back in on repeats. But the newcomers were told, "Come on, load it up, *all* your smokes, son, and give me that watch off your arm, and that ring." We left with at least fifteen sacks full of food, cigarettes and jewelry. Not until we were back in Cellblock 5 did a guard show up on the scene asking if everything had cooled down. He was told that everything was cool but there was a pretty sick fish passed out in Quarantine. After he left to check it out, we could hear the guys in 4 yelling to him: "They robbed us, those motherfuckers, they creamed us." The screw told them he thought they were exaggerating, and they'd be better off forgetting the whole thing.

So Cellblock 5 was victorious again. Instead of getting thrown in the Hole for our violence, that night we partied with $500 worth of smokes, candy, Kool-Aid, potato and taco chips, cocoa and the instant coffee that we'd pillaged, and made deals for the rings and watches that were part of the booty. From then on, the fishes in Quarantine had trouble keeping their canteen. They'd go to the store, get their weekly supply of goodies, and get zapped when they came down the main corridor toward the unit. It didn't matter how big or small he was, the average fish got ripped off. Only if he was an old-timer was he let go. Sometimes the fish would put up a fight, but it would be madness to try and do battle with ten dudes at once. The guards continued to look the other way. I guess they figured that if those hardass cons in 5 were keeping themselves happy taking away canteens, then they wouldn't be hassling *them*. In the fourteen years I was at the pen, there were many turnovers in Cellblock 5 residents, but they always carried on in the same bulldog manner.

And they did it stoned. Most of the cons in Cellblock 5 stayed high on some kind of drug seven days a week. Drugs in the joint were no problem at all, especially for these guys. If you had cash, there was always some underpaid guard eager to make a fast buck and ready to supply you with whatever you needed. And there was a lot of green money floating around the penitentiary: smuggled in during visits, through the legal mail, or via an inmate coming in from the honor unit. Lots of new arrivals who were wise would "kista-stash" (hide in their rectum) their cash. They got away with it because in New Mexico there weren't any probing cavity checks, perhaps because the Catholic upbringing of the mostly Chicano administration, and their macho ethic, made such precautions repugnant.

A bag of grass costing $25 on the street went for $150 in the joint. You could likewise buy heroin or acid. Cocaine was rarer to come by. Commercial booze was also available from guards, but if you weren't flush there was always homebrew, the staple intoxicant of every prison. Cellblock 5 always had a steady supply of home-brew coming in. It could be made anywhere, though in the kitchen most naturally, since that's where all the ingredients were. The fixings could be smuggled up to the dormitories or cellblocks and put together there. When I worked in the kitchen, we'd take a gallon of either raw potatoes, tomato puree, raisins, or anything else that was available, and let it ferment in something large like a five-gallon milk can, filling it with two-thirds of water and ten pounds of sugar. Then we'd mix in raw rising dough or yeast from the bakery to get the brew cooking, stir all of that together, cover it and put it in a warm place for three or four days until it was ready. It tasted about as good as the ingredients sound, but in the joint it seemed as fine as champagne.

When I came back on a new conviction after being paroled in 1974, I decided it was time I grew up. The prison had gotten even worse. It was so overcrowded that there weren't enough jobs or programs to keep the inmates even minimally occupied. Idleness was the major activity. Hundreds of men sat around the dayrooms and dormitories all day long with nothing to do but shoot the shit and scheme on how to get one over on The Man or how to work over some personal or racial enemy. Besides the idle time, the sardine-like living conditions were giving the cons a lot to be angry about.

Researchers at the Yale School of Medicine did a study that proved scientifically, in case no one had noticed the real-life proof, the dangerous effects of overcrowded dormitories in prison. They found that inmates living in this situation experienced an increase in blood pressure, that overcrowding caused stress and tension and required a "high degree of vigilance by inmates,"[2] which involved a loss of personal control and disrupted social relationships. The most natural way to express the frustration was to find a scapegoat. Prison, it's often said, is a reflection of society, and society isn't finished with its racial prejudices. Those prejudices had rubbed off on every convict when he was on the streets, and he carried them into the prison with him, where the pressure made his bigotry a mountain of resentment. Seldom were there out-and-out race wars with ten or more members of each clique fighting each other. Most often clique grudges were carried out in one-to-one stabbings. The majority of the bigotry battles were waged by attitude and talk. And organization.

The rising crime rate had brought more whites and blacks into the penitentiary. By 1980, 53 percent of the population was Chicano/Hispanic, 37 percent Anglo, 9 percent black and 1 percent Indian. The edge was not just in population numbers for Chicanos. Most of the prison personnel were of Hispanic origin. In the early days, when 75 percent of the inmates were Chicano, The Man looked on them as ordinary convict scum and treated them like the same pieces of dirt as the other convicts. Now that the administration and guards had scapegoats not only for their pretensions of self-righteousness but for their racial prejudices as well, they began to show favoritism toward their Chicano brothers. This didn't make the Anglos, once allies, feel any too safe with the Chicano clique. Though there had been a white clique all along, it wasn't until 1973, when bikers from the west coast began to get busted in New Mexico for running drugs cross-country, that the hardcore Aryan Brotherhood began to get a grip on the whites. The bikers reacted strongly to being the underdog to, as they would say, "an inferior race of Mexicans." They also got a lot of heat from everyone in the joint—Chicanos, blacks, the administration, even some whites—because everyone was leery of the ominous and infamous legend of bikers. They decided to form their own group, a prison motorcycle club without the choppers, to be sure their backs were covered in case any of their numerous enemies decided to be brave. As the California bikers began to come into the prison in greater numbers, they started touting the Aryan Brotherhood. "Why just form a clique for bikers," they argued, "there's power in numbers, let's get the A.B. in and all the white bros in the joint can join." They wrote to the California headquarters of the American Nazi Party for the right to open a chapter in the Penitentiary of New Mexico, got permission, and soon just about every white con in the place was a full-fledged member. For the first time in the prison's history, the whites had a clique to equal the long-standing Mexican Mafia of the Chicanos. The blacks, the brunt of both cliques' hatred, got themselves aligned with the Black Muslims; the more politically oriented Black Panthers never gained a foothold in Santa Fe, as they had in most other American prisons, because here blacks were in the minority.

Most of the convicts who belonged to these cliques were not only uneducated, they looked down on anyone who tried to better themselves. They aimed to make everyone believe they were cold, bad motherfuckers, and their attitude was: "No bad motherfucker would go to school." They all cited bigotry of one kind or another as the reason they were in the joint. The blacks thought they were there because of their color. The Chicanos said they were there because of the Anglos, who'd been oppressing Hispanics since they invaded their land a hundred years ago. The whites said they wouldn't be in the joint if they'd had the bucks for high-powered attorneys. Most of them were unwilling to take any responsibility for their situation. They'd talk about the unfairness of society and The Man, but never admit to playing the same game when they infringed on a new convict's freedom by hassling him for protection money or a piece of ass. Let a guard put them in the Hole for some of their carryings on, though, and they'd be the first to snivel that they were being treated unfairly.

I criticize them like an ex-alcoholic criticizes a drunkard, because watching them was like watching a part of myself I wanted to forget. I'm not excusing society for its part in shaping a criminal or denying that the prison administration destroys a man's morale and often his mind. But I'm not letting the clique heavies off the hook either; they do just as much to stop growth and keep anger festering. It's from their ranks that the cruelest rioters came, the ones who would commit atrocities no animal but the human would think of.

# 5

*The last time I went to see him, my brother asked him, when will you be getting out of here? And he said, I think the time I get out of here will be in a coffin.*

—Mother of Joe Madrid, Inmate #25940, Penitentiary of New Mexico[1]

## 2:15 A.M., Saturday, February 2, 1980.

"What's goin'on?" a captain of the Black Muslims asked when a Chicano rioter unlocked his cell door.

Before he could step out, three white militants moved in front of the opened doorway and answered: "Brother, this is a riot. You got five minutes to talk to your people and find out if they're with us or not."

The Muslim nodded mutely and the militants turned and left Cellhouse 6. When the Muslim captain walked out onto the catwalk, he saw that the only other inmates the three white militants had released were the few Chicanos and whites housed in this predominately black cellhouse.

"All right, brothers," he yelled, cranking open the Muslim cell doors as he made his announcement. "As you can see, this is a riot, and whitey and the Mex want to know if we're with them or against them in this shit. Some of you gotta go spread the word to the other brothers on the South side. Tell them we're gonna meet in here—in five, man, these dudes are anxious."

There was no ceiling separating the first and second tiers of the cellhouse, so everyone in the unit could hear his booming voice. Some of the blacks went out into the prison to get their brothers, others went up to the second tier and started unlocking those cell doors. Soon the second tier dayroom and catwalk were filled with every black in the prison except those locked up in Protection. The Muslim captain stood in the middle of the noisy crowd of men, raising voice and hands to quiet them.

"Listen, brothers—you see what's comin' down. Now, what do we do, stay out or get into it? I think if we don't get in it we'll have to get down with every whitey and Mex in this joint. I'd rather raise hell with The Man..."

The crowd shouted their agreement.

"...BUT," he boomed over the uproar, "we've got to make this unit and the old men's dormitory our territorial line. If we spread too thin, whitey might want

38

to fuck with some of our brothers. And one more thing: our minister is in Protection. We have to make getting him out of there our first priority. Once the mob gets in there, there's gonna be deep trouble and we don't want him messed with." He stopped because movement at the door caught his eye.

Ten Aryan brothers and twice as many of the Mexican Mafia were coming into the vestibule at the front of the unit. Some of them were standing on the stairs, blocking the exit. They looked as if they were ready to go to war then and there if they got the wrong answer to the question one of them yelled: "Well, what's it gonna be?"

"Count us in," the Muslim leader said loudly. "My people are as tired of The Man fucking us over as you are, it's payback time all right. There's just one deal we have to make."

"What's that?"

"We want to get Jeff Brewster out of Protection when you get in there—and I mean we want to be the *first* to enter and get him the fuck out before anything comes down."

The militant spokesmen in the front lines looked at each other for silent advice, and nodded back approval. "Okay with us," the leader said out loud.

"Well, we're with you then. You need us, you'll always find someone right here, 'cause this is gonna be our headquarters."

For this night at least, there was peace among the races; peace for the sake of a greater war.

The rioters who'd gone back to the control center to look for the keys to Cellblock 3 were having trouble finding them in the debris. In their impatience to get their friends out of lockup, the group waiting at the cellblock door decided to go down to the basement and get Officer Mendoza; they'd seen him run there after refusing to open the upstairs grill. They demanded that he open *this* gate, which led to the maximum detention units, the bottom tier of Cellblock 3. But once again Officer Mendoza refused.

"Let's go get us a hostage to make him change his mind, what say, bro?"

The bro's agreed and off they went to Dormitory E-2, returning soon with Captain Roybal, who they slammed up against the bars of the locked grill.

"Okay, Mendoza, if you're brave enough to take a look from your hiding place, you'll see we've got your old Captain Roybal here. He ain't very comfortable, he's been beaten pretty bad. This shank we're holding to his throat's only gonna make him feel worse, 'cause if you don't open the door, Mendoza, we're gonna slit his head off his shoulders and roll it down the aisle."

Officer Mendoza didn't have to make a decision.

"Hey, man, fuck those pigs, we found the keys," a Chicano rioter announced, running up to the group. "They were buried under a ton of shit down there. Someone must've knocked 'em down when we tore it apart."

They fumbled with the keys and had difficulty finding the right one. In that small interim, three guards came out of their hiding closet and locked themselves behind another grill. When the rioters finally succeeded in unlocking the gate and were inside, the officers surrendered. They were roughed up, hit across the legs with pipes, spit on, cursed at, but their treatment was nowhere near as brutal as that of the first seven captured guards. These three officers were ordered to strip naked, then they were shoved into a cell and locked in. They remained there for the duration of the riot.

"Hey, what's goin' on out there?" a voice called from one of the maximum detention units.

Maximum detention units have solid steel doors with no windows, so the inmate inside could only hear that there was more noise than usual. Perhaps he didn't believe his ears when he heard the answer shouted back.

"It's a riot, man, we've taken over the joint. Who're you?"

"Primi Martinez. Far out, let me outta this fuckin' hole so I can join in, will ya?"

"*Ohhh*—good old Archie Martinez, eh?"

"Primi baby, is that really you all locked up in that dungeon, Primi Martinez, the king of the snitches? Nah, man, we're not gonna let you out. We're gonna come in there and show you how much we appreciate all you've done for us, Primi. You know what we mean, so you can *really* feel it, right down to your prick."

There was silence from the cell. Primi Martinez was busy jamming his toothbrush in the crack of his door so it couldn't be cranked open. Just in time, too. The rioters were in front of his cell as he got it in place. When the crank wouldn't move, they demanded he open the door.

"Fuck you, no way," he answered, his tone more surly than fearful.

"If you don't, we're gonna do you real bad when we do get in there, and we'll get in, Primi, so make your confession, bro, 'cause your day has come."

Most of this was said in their native language, but being a homeboy wasn't going to save Archie Martinez. He was the biggest snitch in the joint. There were a lot of men in Cellblock 3 who he'd put there, and a lot of rioters he'd informed on. They vowed they'd be back with some of these men, and better weapons, to deal with him. Specifically they had in mind a blowtorch they knew was kept in the basement plumbing shop.

The group moved along the hallway, asking who was inside each of the units as they went. They unlocked three or four inmates who were from general population. But when they heard the name Juan Sanchez, someone remembered that he was "that crazy sonofabitch" that a buddy of theirs had a beef with.

Juan Sanchez was a Mexican national who'd been placed in the Protection unit because he was genuinely insane, not because he was a snitch. Even those in Protection can get thrown in the Hole if they get wild, and Juan Sanchez often got wild. That he hadn't been sent to the loony bin, the forensic unit in Las Vegas, New Mexico, instead of the joint always amazed everyone. From the moment Sanchez had come into the prison, his behavior smacked of derangement. He'd tried to kill himself several times, cutting his arms open with a razor in the first attempt. Then he turned his attacks on other inmates. He would get delusional and talk about seeing visions of the devil and Jesus Christ. All this earned him a label—paranoid schizophrenic—from the psych department, plus lockup, first in Cellblock 3, then in the Protection unit. It also brought the wrath of the guards, who would beat him up constantly for no good reason except that they were tired of his babbling. In March of 1979, he complained to the administration that his sink was stopped up. Their response was to call the goon squad, who did their usual lesson-teaching routine, hitting him in the back, ribs and head with their clubs before throwing him into the Hole. Naked, of course. Juan Sanchez might have been crazy, but he had enough marbles to write a letter to the Mexican Consulate shortly thereafter, in May of 1979, asking to be transferred to Mexico as part of the U.S.-Mexico prisoner transfer treaty happening at the time. "The officials of the institution and the prisoners are torturing me," his letter began. A fight with another prisoner, he wrote, had caused an inmate to threaten to kill him. "How are you going to kill me when we are locked in separate cells in Cellblock 3?" he had asked the inmate. "He said he was going to take my life and has played cards and never lost a game." The inmate began harassing him, calling him a *gallina* (coward) and *joto* (homosexual). In fact, when he wrote the Consulate, both prisoners *and* prison officials taunted him about his courage and his manhood. "I heard on the official loudspeaker that I had confessed to the gringos and Chicanos that I was a coward and a homosexual…They were playing with my honor as a man, torturing me mentally, withholding food, trying to humiliate me."[2] But the Mexican Consulate didn't take immediate enough action to save Juan Sanchez.

A rioter armed with a tear gas gun opened the windowless cell door and walked in. Juan Sanchez was standing in a corner mumbling to himself. The light let in by the opened door blinded him, unaccustomed as he was to anything but darkness, so he didn't see the rioter approach and fire a teargas canister into his face. Maybe he didn't even feel his head explode. Maybe Juan Sanchez died peacefully with the help of his delusional angels.

His murderer and the small band of rioters with him turned their attention to the main goal: Freeing their buddies upstairs in Cellblock 3. They dragged the naked and badly battered Captain Roybal along with them instead of returning him to Dormitory E-2. This was a smart move on their part. They had the key to the unit's main grill, but the gates at the entrance of each row of cells were controlled by a panel they didn't know how to operate. A shank was held to Captain Roybal's throat once again as he was forced to show them how the panel worked. When the first tier was opened, four or five of the men ran down the corridors shouting the good news and cranking open cell doors. The inmates in the cellblock began whooping and yelling.

"Hurry up, bro, let's get this goddamned grill open so I can get out of here."

"We've got work to do, it's about time we fucked up this place!"

Their uproar could be heard all over the north side of the prison. Many of these men had been in lock-up for six months or more. The prospect of getting out of their cells and having the freedom to walk around would have been enough to excite them, but the added incentive of revenge made their blood boil.

While these inmates were being released, the rest of this liberating band of rioters dragged Roybal up to the third tier and forced him to show them how to operate *that* control panel. They rewarded him by locking him in the first cell opened. He stayed there for the duration of the riot, naked, no doubt cold and, as he listened to the convicts going wild as they were set free, wondering if he'd ever come out of this alive.

A Lieutenant of the Aryan Brotherhood, one of the original riot instigators from Dormitory E-2, ran up and down the aisles looking for two of his close buddies, also bikers and honchos in the Brotherhood. They'd been in lock-up since being captured after their December breakout with nine other escapees. When he found one, the first words out of his friend's mouth were: "Well, bro, looks like you guys finally got your shit together. Hurry up and get the door open so I can get the fuck out of this sonofabitch." The lieutenant obliged, and the two of them went down the corridor until they came to the third member of this triumvirate and cranked open his door. These three stayed close while they helped their other bros unlock all the whites in Segregation.

Meanwhile, the Chicanos were busy unlocking their clique, and the blacks theirs, until all eighty-six inmates in lock-up, men the administration labeled as the most dangerous in the prison, were free. Most of the fourteen-member execution squad—a squad that would soon deal death to those they judged guilty of crimes against the convict ethic—came from among these inmates. It was a well-integrated clique: Chicanos, whites and blacks were all represented in this execution squad.

Once the Aryan Brotherhood had all been freed, they huddled in the middle tier of the cellblock.

"The first thing we have to do is get ourselves some real weapons," one of the leaders said. "And the best place to get them is in the kitchen..."

"The next thing we gotta get is the snitches," another interrupted, gathering noisy agreement from his colleagues.

"Right on, so let's fuckin' *go!*"

The group stormed down the corridor to the kitchen and broke into the steward's office, where they knew the knives were locked in a cabinet at night. In ten minutes they had the cabinet open and themselves armed with butcher knives and meat cleavers. These weapons didn't go unused for long. On the way out of the kitchen, the biker triumvirate bumped into a one-armed old-timer who had once refused to join the Aryan Brotherhood. When the three saw him, they decided to give him his payback. Pointing their knives at his throat and belly, they told him to get up against the wall. He did as he was told, but his obedience didn't save him. He was slammed on the head with a meat cleaver and knocked to the floor.

"Hold him down, man, I've always wanted to fuck a man with no arms."

The biker's two companions complied, while he pulled a long carving knife out of his belt and started sawing through the skin and muscles of the man's only arm. The old-timer wasn't any slouch. Whether through fear or pain, he managed to wriggle and wrestle his way free of the two holding him down and, kneeing his attacker off of him, run for his life down the smoky, crowded corridor. The three didn't bother chasing him; they just laughed.

"Fuck him," one said. "We've got more important shit to take care of."

The one-armed old-timer didn't lose life or limb, but the tendons and muscles were cut so severely that the use of his only arm was forever seriously impaired; a hard way to go in the world, but triply hard in prison.

Bands of rioters in search of weapons and destruction had followed the bikers into the kitchen and were breaking into the storerooms, taking everything that could be used for violence, from rolling pins to cast-iron pans, as well as food to stash in the cells and dorms. They tore the place apart, breaking windows and all the glassware, smashing tables and chairs, pulling out electrical wiring, ripping out the plumbing and flooding the floor. They destroyed everything they could.

Other gangs were wrecking the canteen, taking as much candy, coffee and clothing as they were able to carry, stocking up for the hours, possibly days, they thought the riot might last. Still others were down in the basement raiding the shops for new additions to their arsenal. In the plumbing shop they found the *crème de la crème* of weapons, a heavy-duty acetylene cutting torch. And in the paint and shoe repair shops they discovered large quantities of the favorite high of many of the convicts: "Sniff—paint, paint thinner and glue. The drugs found in the hospital were mainly downers that should have made the inmates more mellow than violent; but mixed with "sniff," known to induce ferocious behavior, the tranquilizers became energizers.

The group that found the acetylene cutting torch dragged it upstairs to the end of the south side corridor, where the Educational Unit and Dormitory D were. These units were closed off from the rest of the prison by a grill the rioters hadn't found a key for. The rioter holding the torch turned it on the bars of the grill until it cut them open. The eighty-six residents of the dormitory, some of whom were new arrivals housed in the orientation or quarantine units of the dorm, were released, but the torch-bearers took Officer Michael Hernandez, who'd hidden himself in the educational section, as hostage. Hernandez was twenty-five years old and had only been at the institution for four months. He was initiated into prisoner violence by feeling their pipes and clubs beating down on him. Fortunately for Hernandez, the rioters were anxious to get on with other massacres and didn't spend a lot of time assaulting him. With the release of Dormitory D, every inmate in the institution was free to roam the prison. That is, every inmate except the ninety-six men locked up in Cellblock 4, the Protection Unit.

Down the corridor from Dormitory D, an angry mob had gathered outside the door of the semi-protection unit, E-1. The residents of E-1 had barricaded themselves in. They were younger men who had problems being in general population, problems like getting raped and harassed for money. They needed protection not because they were snitches but because they were not able to grow the teeth it takes to survive in the convict jungle. They didn't need to be caged in lone cells twenty-four hours a day. They were neither troublemakers nor inform-ers, but whenever they ventured out into the main corridor they were escorted by guards, and though they ate in the mess hall, it was at a different time than the rest of the population. These were men who just wanted to serve their time and get out without being touched by the cruelty they'd experienced in the main-stream of prison life. In the eyes of most convicts, however, they were simply weak. Many of these inmates had enemies among the population, and all of them knew that by choosing their protected status they were despised. They were therefore naturally leery of the coaxing words being spoken by the rioters outside their barricaded door.

"Hey now, why don't you guys take that shit down and come on out and join us."

"As far as being mad at you, we're not. Let bygones be bygones."

"We're all together now, and all we want to do is fight The Man."

Their refusal infuriated the mob.

"You sons-of-bitches either come out now or we're gonna come in and drag you out, and if we have to do that, we're gonna fuck up a whole bunch of you real bad."

"Fuck you," someone from inside the unit yelled out. "We're not leavin'. You want us, you come on in and get us if you can."

The door was solid on the bottom, but the upper half had twelve six-by-eight-foot wire-meshed windows in it. The rioters began pummeling the windows with pipes and clubs until there were jagged holes in several of them. Someone aimed a tear-gas gun at one of the openings, hoping, of course, that the canister would fall into the unit and choke the men inside. Instead, it bounced off the door and into the corridor, exploding in the midst of the aggressors, who moved away, cough-ing and cursing. But when the gas cleared enough for them to deal with it, they came back, more determined now to have their way. By the sheer weight of a group push they attempted to shove the door open, but succeeded only in creat-ing a four or five inch gap. Beyond that, the barricade of bunk beds, tables and chairs held. One of the rioters tried crawling through this small opening, but as soon as he stuck his arm in, an E-1 resident slammed a chair leg on it hard enough to break the intruder's wrist.

"Sonofabitch! You broke my arm! I'll kill you, you no good cocksucker!"

The rioters conferred. Someone got the bright idea to smoke them out. Drag-ging blankets, mattresses, newspapers and pillows in front of the door, they set fire to them, but this time, too, their plan failed. The men in E-1 were ready, and fanned the smoke back out into the corridor. Once again their tormenters had to disperse for air.

Among this group of rioters was an inmate named Joe Madrid. He wasn't mad at anyone in E-1. In fact, he had a few friends in the unit. He'd been talking to one of those friends earlier, trying to convince him that it would be better all around for them to come out. Now he understood his friend's reticence. While the rest of the mob was off trying to find a place to breathe, Joe called over the barricade to his buddy.

"Listen, I think the best thing for you guys to do is get outside the prison and give yourselves up to The Man."

"Yeah, that's a good idea, Joe, but how? We don't have anything in here we can get the windows out with."

"A pipe wrench will do it. I'll go find one in one of the shops downstairs. I'll be back."

In a few minutes, Joe returned with a three-foot wrench. As he was handing it to his friend through the opening in the barricade, the rioters were returning and saw the transaction.

"Hey, you sonofabitch," one of them called to Joe. "If they get out because of you, your ass is mine."

"Hey, some of those guys in there are my friends, and I don't think they should be hassled," Joe tried to explain to this group of mostly fellow Chicanos.

They were having none of it, and began yelling and shouting curses at him. Finally someone came from behind and hit him over the head with a riot stick. The blow drew blood and knocked Joe to the ground. The gang began attacking him with their pipes and clubs, kicking and beating him mercilessly; beating the life out of him.

"Hey, man, I think he's dead," someone announced.

When the rioters realized that indeed their victim had stopped breathing, they dragged his body the length of the corridor to the gymnasium, where others were busy tearing apart that facility. There they got a fifteen-foot length of rope and used it to demonstrate the proper treatment for the body of a traitor. Joe Madrid had gone against them in favor of the weaklings and, homeboy though he was, that made him a traitor. Tying the rope under his arms and around his chest, they strung him up on the basketball hoop for all to see. There he would hang for the rest of the riot: Joe Madrid, serving a one-to-five year sentence for possession of narcotics, dead at thirty-eight because he tried to be a nice guy in the Penitentiary of the Land of Enchantment. During those hours of madness that were to follow, inmates would come in and hack at his dangling corpse with knives, beat it with pipes, mutilating it so totally that it was beyond recognition, a raw, bloody mass of flesh, by the time the uprising was over.

But then, violence is inherent in the Land of Enchantment, and in the Chicano culture. It's the land of the Penitente, the self-flagellating Catholics of northern New Mexico, who whip themselves in private to scourge the sins of their soul. At Easter, they do one of their sect the honor of crucifying him in an enactment of Christ's death on the cross. This Cristo doesn't die on the cross—no nails are used. Instead, his wrists and feet are tied to the cross, a cross he carries many miles to the crucifixion site while his friends whip him as he walks, just as the Christ he's portraying was tormented along the road to Calvary. Those in the procession are equally penitent, lashing themselves with sticks and whips, and sometimes cactus. Los Hermanos Penitentes is one of the few folk religions alive in the western world today. It developed when the Spanish priests had to leave New Mexico in 1828 because of their nation's dwindling empire. These class-conscious friars had steadfastly resisted taking into the priesthood the mixed-blood natives—the mestizo blend of Spanish, Mexican and Indian. They left behind only a handful of men who were trained in the rituals of the Church, and these serviced the more accessible areas. The people living in the isolated mountain country were left to their own spiritual devices. They chose to worship what they experienced so much of in the cold, stark mountains of the north: Pain and death.

Archie Martinez came from that north country: Chimayo, in the northern mountains of New Mexico. Chimayo is not only Penitente land, it is also known as the "Lourdes of America" because of El Santuario de Chimayo and its healing mud. Travelers from around the world flock there year-round to heal their diseases by spreading the moist sand on their ailing parts. Crutches, leg braces, rosaries, dog tags, driver's licenses, shoes and more all hang on the ancient adobe walls of the Santuario as testimony to the mud's miraculous power. One miracle it did not perform was changing poverty to wealth for Archie Martinez; so he took the matter into his own hands and began robbing his neighbors' houses. He was quite successful at this endeavor, especially because there were no police in the village community. He had talent, too. No matter what traps the villagers would set, Archie Martinez always eluded them. He was so swift and slippery that the townsfolk began to build a legend around him: Archie Martinez could only be escaping them because he turned into a "fleet-footed dog." They called him the Dog Boy of Chimayo.[3]

But every dog has his day, and Archie wound up at the Penitentiary of New Mexico. Even here he tried his "Dog Boy" routine. In the six years he'd been in prison, he tried twice to escape. These attempts only netted him more time: ten to fifty years for the first try, two-to-ten for the second. All this, plus his reputation as king of the snitches, the fleet-footed Dog Boy of Chimayo had accomplished in only twenty-five years of living.

Besides being the king of the snitches, Archie Martinez was cursed with an obnoxious personality. During his first years in population he'd always been in on the rapes of the new young inmates. He and four or five of his bros would pull a train on the guy, take his canteen, then make him pay protection money. But soon his fleet-footedness failed him and his snitching routine hit the grapevine. For the sake of his life's safety he had to spend his time locked up day and night in Protection; or in the Hole. When his big mouth wasn't snitching, it was getting him in trouble with the guards. At the time of the riot, he was in the Hole for cursing and throwing a cup of coffee at one of them.

Now the execution squad, armed with the acetylene cutting torch, came to give Archie his payback for years of informing on them.

"Hey, Arch, we're back. You don't have to open the door, man, we've got a key of our own," they yelled in at him.

At first his response was a surly, "The fuck you do." But when he heard the roar of the torch and felt its heat on the steel door, he changed his attitude. "Look, man, I don't want no trouble. Why do you want me?"

They told him while they were burning through the door, naming instance after instance when they'd been locked up or thrown in the Hole because he'd told The Man about their activities.

He denied it all. "No, man, it wasn't me, I didn't do that, why don't you let me out so I can join you?"

"No, Primi, we want your ass. Did you say those prayers, boy? 'Cause you better make your peace while you can."

"Listen, I'll take the jam off my door, just let me come out on my own, what do you say?"

"Nah, it's more fun this way. Yeah, Primi, we're gonna have some fun with you, baby. We're gonna turn this torch all over your sniveling body, nice and slow so's you can feel it. Then when you're nice and toasted, we'll cut your dick off and let you taste it."

The door fell off the hinges and they pushed it open. Archie Martinez was standing against the far wall clutching a mattress to his naked body. They dragged him out of the cell and upstairs to the first tier of Cellblock 3 while he screamed all the way: *"No era yo, no lo hice,"* ("It wasn't me, I didn't do it"). The execution squad was deaf to his pleas. They handcuffed his arms and legs spread-eagle to the bars of the guard station in front of the cellblock. They were going to make this a public rite of torture and execution. Archie Martinez' screams could be heard not only on the north side but far into the main corridor that ran through the penitentiary. They started by beating him with pipes, riot sticks and chains, breaking his legs, knocking out his teeth and bloodying his face, causing God knows what kind of internal injuries as the clubs hammered his chest and stomach. The beating was so intense that he passed out, but one of the squad went to the hospital and came back with smelling salts, bringing him to consciousness so he could witness the pain of their next torment. Taking a straight razor, they slit the skin over both eyelids and gouged out his eyeballs until they hung down on his cheeks. Again he passed out and again he was brought around with the smelling salts, this time so he could take one last look at the world through his changed perspective; and witness the sudden blackout as they sliced through the optic nerves. The eyeballs fell to the floor and one of the squad picked them up. "Hey, Arch, I got your eyeballs to remember you by," he taunted, running the bottle of salts under his victim's nose. As Archie came to, he pleaded with them to kill him, to let him die, but they laughed. "No, Arch, we got more in store for you." They brought the razor down on his penis and sliced it off. The smelling salts brought him around just as they were jamming it into his already bloodied mouth. Then they turned the acetylene torch on him, slowly burning each part of his body: first his chest, then his stomach, his face, hands, legs, what was left of his genitals, stopping once to administer the smelling salts and bring him to, rotating the torch among themselves.

The fleet-footed Dog Boy of Chimayo would never regain consciousness. The execution squad kept on burning him until they saw he was dead. Then they took his body down and left it lying there for all to see. It was so mutilated that it took hours to find out who it was when the riot was over. But that would be many horror-filled incidents later.

# 6

*The character and mentality of the keepers may be of more importance in understanding prisons than the character and mentality of the kept. Would that the hordes of researchers who now invade the prisons…explore their childhood traumas, flip inkblots to find out what their Rorschach tests reveal, generally try to discover what makes them tick and what made them choose this occupation in the first place. For after all, if we were to ask a small boy, "What do you want to be when you grow up?" and he were to answer, "A prison guard," should we not find that a trifle worrying—cause, perhaps, to take him off to a child guidance clinic for observation and therapy?*

—JESSICA MITFORD[1]

Felix Rodriguez, the granddaddy of corrections in New Mexico, began his career as a guard at the Penitentiary, as did many of his friends. "There was a group of officers there who'd grown up together. These guys came home from the Korean War, and the major industry in Santa Fe was the Department of Corrections. A group of them got in there in 1953, 1954, and stayed there. Felix was the father, the paternal, benevolent dictator of the penitentiary," Tony Anaya, the Attorney General who succeeded in having Rodriguez removed from his position as warden told a reporter after the riot.[2] As is the custom of New Mexico's eternally Democrat-run government and its bag of political party favors, Rodriguez was not thrown out of the Department of Corrections all together. In spite of evidence that he headed an administration heavily involved in drug trafficking and prisoner intimidation, he was given another position in the department, albeit outside the prison. As testament to his power at the time of the 1980 riot, five years after he was ousted Felix Rodriguez was Deputy Secretary of Corrections, the man who ran the whole show. By then he and his cronies were known as the Santa Fe Eleven, the clique that had for twenty years controlled the Penitentiary of New Mexico as if it were their own private empire.[2a]

I'd watched this clique strengthen since I came into the prison in 1962. You might say we all grew tough together. By 1970 the clique had become firmly entrenched in the five top positions inside the penitentiary, and everyone who held an important management post was an active member of it. The only people who kept their jobs were those who played the game the clique's way. The majority of prison personnel, including all the top five members, were Chicano. Nepotism, that familiar abuse of power, kept it that way. Anyone with a plum position was related to or a friend of someone high up in the administration. To wit, in 1971, Warden Rodriguez's administrative assistant married a personnel technician at the institution. Not only could they talk to each other about work over supper; at family gatherings they could discuss it with the administrative assistant's brother, who was the business manager, as well as with the brother's nephew, the prison storekeeper.[3] If by chance a man who wasn't well connected got hired, he'd end up with night shift in the guard tower, the worst job in the prison, until he proved he was willing to play according to the clique's rules.

Felix Rodriguez, the leader of the clique, started in the prison system in 1955 and worked his way up through the ranks, from guard to lieutenant to associate warden to deputy warden. It was in this last position that he began to assume the power he'd been building throughout the years, for in Santa Fe it was the deputy warden who actually ran the penitentiary. When Rodriguez became warden in 1970, he secured the muscle of his clique by promoting tried and trusted cronies to the four deputy and associate warden positions. In spite of their bitter feelings about this clique, the convicts respected Rodriguez himself. He was fair, his word could be trusted, and he was never one to side only with the guards. If he thought there was merit to an inmate's complaint, he'd call the officer in, listen to both stories, and be as likely to reprimand the guard as he would the inmate. Rodriguez had other aspects, however, which put him in the same category as the rest of his henchmen. He had a tendency to throw temper tantrums and to hold grudges. If he thought a convict was scheming to deal drugs or stash weapons, or if he caught him at it, or even if he just didn't like the con's attitude, he'd keep him on his blacklist forever. No matter how good the inmate's record might become, he wouldn't be able to get a job, a cellblock change, or enroll in an educational program. And Rodriguez always knew who was doing what. The snitch system was his baby, and he kept it running smoothly with promises of privileges and threats of none. He soft-pedaled the phenomenon to the press: "You have to establish your network so that you're informed about everything that is happening. Most prisoners want to do their time in the easiest way possible and don't want trouble. Some of the intelligence, or information, that comes from prisoners is a result of that desire for quiet."[4] Quiet my butt—the only quiet an informer got was relief from the flack the administration would give him if he didn't snitch.

Rodriguez and his clique were as avid in maintaining their power and their snitch circuits as they were their philosophy that punishment was the way to rehabilitate the criminal mind. Only for ten months in its long history did the Penitentiary of New Mexico have at its helm an inmate-oriented warden, and the shortness of his term speaks for the difficulty he had in establishing his humane policies. Rodriguez had been acting-warden for the year it took to find a new man to follow Harold Cox, who'd been in the top position for seven years. When J.E. Baker came into the institution in 1968, Rodriguez went back to being deputy warden. This time, however, he had trouble wielding his usual power. Warden Baker had ideas of his own as well as the strength to impose them on his unwilling staff. The most radical change he made was the abolition of the maximum detention unit as a disciplinary vehicle. Though Rodriguez and his group argued that punishment was an integral part of keeping the inmates under control, Baker stuck to his plan and closed down the Hole. This made a lot of the officers unhappy, but the convicts began to see that not all representatives of law enforcement were pigs. That is not to say they didn't take undue advantage of the new liberality and give the guards a bad time: Often they did, for revenge is sweet. They knew nothing serious was going to happen any more if they were written up for an infraction of the rules, that the threats the officers made were hollow, for they had no means of carrying them out. If an inmate felt a guard was treating him unfairly, he knew he could go over his head straight to Warden Baker and find a sympathetic ear. This gave the convicts leeway to bait the guards, to speak their minds more freely. Consequently, during this period there was a large turnover in prison personnel. These guards had not been trained even for a job as a jailer, no less for one in which they had to use psychology and man-to-man humanity in the treatment of their prisoners.

Baker didn't just take away punishment, he instituted educational programs geared to teach an inmate something besides making license plates, programs that would help ease an ex-felon's re-entry into society by providing him with marketable abilities. He brought college education into the prison, making it available to all convicts, not just those few the administration deemed ready to travel outside the institution to attend classes at the College of Santa Fe. He initiated Project Newgate, a program that tutored inmates who wanted to get into the college classes but needed more study to meet the scholastic requirements for entrance.

Rodriguez and his clique had the last word however. Baker took over as warden just after the 1968 legislative session ended. It would be ten months before they would meet again to take up the business of confirming his appointment. In that interim, the press and legislators heard about the liberal changes Baker had been making. Knowing their constituency didn't like politicians who were soft on crime, the legislature told Baker he was going too fast too soon; the state couldn't afford the money he was asking them to spend on Corrections, and therefore they could not agree to keep him on as warden. They gave the job to Felix Rodriguez.

The inmates' frustration over the reinstitution of the punishment philosophy of Rodriguez and his clique boiled over in 1971. In spite of the fact that a grand jury report in July of that year suggested that the vocational training facilities should be made available to more inmates, the clique continued their use of these programs as rewards for good behavior, which meant the willingness to supply information. And in spite of the fact that the same grand jury report urged the hiring of a full-time resident psychiatrist "who is particularly trained in the areas of criminal psychology, narcotics counseling, and alcoholism..." none was sought, no less hired. The convicts therefore had no help and much hindrance in adjusting to the switch from being treated like humans to being handled like animals. When the riot at Attica came down in September 1971, they were inspired to raise their own voices in protest and a month later staged a work strike that wasn't all together peaceful. Several dormitories were torn apart before the protest was quelled by police and tear gas.

To Rodriguez's credit he did later interview many of the strikers to hear their complaints about conditions. He was a good enough politician to act on what he heard. In the interest of keeping peace in the prison and the public's eye off his domain, Rodriguez opened up the educational and vocational training to more than just his snitches. Cons also had incentives for maintaining the status quo, especially those who had jobs and were participating in classes, along with those who ran the drug-dealing rackets. They didn't want any waves made either and were instrumental in keeping the rest of the population quiet during the coming years. Dealing drugs in prison during those days was easy. I had a nice money-making hustle going on, getting marijuana smuggled in and selling it at a dollar a joint. As long as I didn't get in The Man's way, I knew my operation was safe.

For four more years this went on while Rodriguez and his tight little clique ruled the penitentiary. Then, in 1975, just a year after the election of a new progressive Governor and an ambitious Attorney General, their power preserve was ruptured. Attorney General Tony Anaya had been elected to that office on the heels of a man who had brought more than a taint of corruption to it, and he was determined to restore integrity to the position. When allegations of loan sharking, drug trafficking, and bookmaking were made against the prison hospital administrator, Frank Stockham, Anaya launched a full-scale investigation into the matter. Observers in the media considered this move a purely political one because Stockham had just been recommended for a promotion by his friend of many years, the new Governor, Jerry Apodaca. The complaint against Stockham, who was not one of the clique, had been lodged by Rodriguez's top men in response to the Governor's recommendation. The Attorney General's investigation showed, however, that Rodriguez's men had done a bit more than simply *file* the complaint; they had in fact framed it through the use of their snitches. The report told the public what we on the inside had always known: That there had indeed been a "clique that has run the penitentiary for a number of years...As much as the inmates use one another, they are also being used by some prison officials."[5] There was, however, no evidence to support the *criminal* charges leveled against the hospital administrator. Though Stockham admitted that he'd taken drugs from the hospital for his personal use, and that his loose control had made it possible for the inmates to have easy access to drugs, only this allegation was proven:

> It appears Stockham was attempting to assist an inmate secure money from his mother in order to pay gambling debts to other inmates. There was fear for the inmate's safety from the threat of his fellow inmates to whom he owed money. Despite his humanitarian motives, this action violates penitentiary rules.

Because of this violation, the Rodriguez clique had its way and Stockholm was fired. This didn't take the heat off of them, however. The report went on to say:

> It is the conclusion of the Attorney General's office that each senior corrections and penitentiary administrative official is responsible to some degree for the hasty and unprofessional manner in which the Stockham report was put together and for acting on a report which was of highly questionable reliability. The warden and deputy warden should be each held responsible for failing to conduct a more thorough and professional investigation and for the use of hopes and promises or the veiled promises, of early parole board, changes in working conditions, or changes in living conditions in the penitentiary to secure false statements.[6]

The report detailed the "investigation" the administration had conducted to make their charges of drug trafficking and more against Stockham, saying it consisted of information from five convicts and one prison employee:

> Four of the five received preferential treatment (such as being moved to trustee status or better work detail). All of them testified they knew they

would be rewarded for statements made against Stockham and punished if they did not give derogatory statements.

The Attorney General concluded the report by noting that though drug-trafficking was not found in Frank Stockham's case, there was unchecked entry of heroin, cocaine, cash, and liquor into the prison; and that the Stockham affair:

> …has highlighted the manner in which corrections and penitentiary officials can manipulate employees and inmates to serve their own selfish interests."[7]

As a result, the corrections secretary was fired. Warden Rodriguez, along with a deputy warden, the chief security officer and an associate warden were removed from their jobs inside the penitentiary. These four, however, were transferred to other positions within the state's Department of Corrections, where they all remained in top management well beyond the 1980 riot.

With the ousting of the main members of the clique, the inmates had high hopes that the new Governor, the first Chicano to be elected to the state's highest office in fifty-four years, was going to change the quality of prison life. Those hopes soared when his newly appointed corrections secretary hired as his administrative aid a hardcore ex-con, a man who'd spent twelve years in the penitentiary, two of them on Death Row, on a first-degree murder conviction that had been commuted to life when the state's death penalty was found unconstitutional. He was the only inmate I've seen in all my years in the pen who used his time not only to educate himself but to totally transform his way of thinking. Unfortunately, the hiring of this ex-con was the only progressive prison event in Governor Apodaca's term. It hadn't been a bed of roses under the Rodriguez clan, but what was to come made it look like it had been.

The new warden was not the great white hope everyone expected. Ralph Aaron, an ex-federal warden with thirty years in corrections under his belt, came in with the hard-line attitude that the institution had gone to hell and he was going to take control because the inmates were running the place. Unlike Rodriguez, who would at least give a con a fair hearing, Aaron treated the inmates as if they were lucky to be breathing. As sparsely as Rodriguez had doled out educational projects during his reign, under Warden Aaron they were practically nil. All programs that took an inmate outside the prison were closed down. Project Newgate folded because no one had bothered to seek funding for it.[7a] Gone now were the incentives—even the illegal ones—that had kept inmates in line for the past four years. The Attorney General's report on the Rodriguez clique had brought the state police in to check the drug flow into the prison. This cut down on the rackets, though it didn't entirely eradicate them; they had, after all, been flourishing during the old regime and many of the prison personnel who had been involved in them were still working in the institution. "Not only were the guards aware, for example, of the narcotics trafficking," Attorney General Tony Anaya told a reporter, "but some of the guards and some of the higher-ups had to be actually participating in the actual trafficking itself. It simply could not go on to the extent that it was going on without the actual involvement by officials."[8]

Though Warden Aaron's clampdown and tight security measures made it difficult to get drugs and to make a comfortable prison living from their sale, his attempts to clean up the penitentiary were frustrated at every turn. Answering a question by a newsperson as to whether he found that guards had been bringing drugs into the prison during his administration, Aaron said: "Yes, we found there were several. We had a problem. We talked with officials downtown about it. I was told at a later date, not too long before I resigned: 'Don't worry about it; particularly if the guy was Chicano, you're not going to get him convicted.'"[9] It was this attitude, together with the fact that his strict ideas about security procedures were not being carried out (years later he told of watching an officer leave a meeting about security regulations, walk down the corridor and casually slide open and *leave* open every grill he passed through), that made Aaron quit just six months after he started. However, he managed to hand pick his successor: Clyde Malley.

Clyde Malley's zeal for security was as strong as his predecessor's, but he was as ineffectual in changing the laxness of the guards as Aaron had been. In fact, during the combined seventeen months the two of them held the office of warden at the penitentiary, there were nineteen escapes, more than there had been in the past ten years. The frustrated Malley attributed one of those escapes to "a complete breakdown of security, established procedures, misinformation, lack of responsible leadership, and general chaos. In thirty years in corrections, I have never witnessed such a total breakdown of basic prison practices."[10] If this carelessness was the guards' way of saying they weren't satisfied with conditions, with being underpaid and under-trained correction officers, the inmates echoed the feeling about their own conditions, and found their way of expressing it. Not only did the outside educational programs remain discontinued, but in his attempt at greater security, Malley had removed all convicts from their administrative positions in the remaining programs, returning them to the idleness that was fast becoming the most abundant occupation in the institution. The convict's mind is never idle, however. Thinking is one of the few rights that can't be taken from him.

During the spring of 1976, the residents at Santa Fe spent their free time scheming on ways to get the administration to change their tune. They knew the only effective means of doing that was to catch the public's attention. This meant staging some kind of uprising to protest conditions, which were intolerable from every point of view. Besides Malley's oppressive regime, the institution was infested with rats and cockroaches, the toilets didn't work, and the food was, as usual, bad. Back and forth through the vents went talk about what kind of action to take. It was decided that the entire population would stage a sit-down strike while the warden had a chance to look over a list of grievances and demands they would compile and present to him. They were agreed that if the administration didn't show signs of giving in on at least some points on the list, they would launch an all-out riot and tear the prison apart. The strike leaders wrote up their tabulation of gripes and remedies and passed word through the vent grapevine that they were ready to go. On the morning of Flag Day, Monday, June 14, 1976, everyone remained in their housing units and refused to go to work or meals until their complaints were answered. By noon the administration sent word: "We're tired of your game, you either go to the mess hall tonight or we're coming in to lock you up." No compromises, no mention of our grievances. The inmates didn't budge either, and The Man did as he promised: locked all cell-block residents in their "houses" and secured the gates to the dormitory units. Those in the cellblocks couldn't do much damage, but the five hundred inmates housed in the dormitories carried out their plan and tore their units apart. Four of the prison's five dorms were demolished before the riot was brought under control by guards with tear gas. No one was taken hostage, no one was seriously hurt, and none of the grievances or demands was even discussed. All that was accomplished by this outbreak was more punishment.

After the tear gassing, six hundred inmates were taken, twenty or thirty at a time, and forced to strip naked and stand in the main corridor while lines of guards and prison personnel on either side questioned them to find out who the strike leaders were. Of course no one talked. No convict was going to snitch in front of his fellows, and the administration had to know this. The interrogation could only have been designed for the purposes of humiliation and retribution; as was the axe-handle gauntlet that followed. As the buck-naked inmates were made to run—on their way to the gym—between the two lines of corrections personnel, they were smacked on the butt, head, back and arms by officers wielding large axe handles. Some convicts were hurt seriously enough to warrant being sent to the infirmary for stitches, others suffered broken knees and elbows, and all suffered yet another loss of self-esteem. One of these axe-handle wielders was a member of the church. He was hated by the inmates because he catered to the "short eyes," those who were child molesters and sex offenders, the most despised convicts in any prison. They were, in fact, the only men who attended services in his chapel. He was a sight, going around to all the dormitories after this axe-handle scene, preaching a hell and brimstone sermon to excuse his actions. He'd done it for God, of course, and everyone deserved everything that was happening to them, bad conditions and all. What he and the prison administration had been trying to do, he explained, was "get the devil out of you." From that time on, he became known as "Axehandle." During the 1980 riot, the cons gave him his payback by burning down a chapel.

Warden Malley never made an effort to talk to inmates about their complaints. His only concern was finding and punishing the strike leaders. Those he believed to be the instigators he placed in Segregation and kept them there for months, even years, according to the Attorney General's report on the incident.[11] Others were transferred out of the prison to another state to insure the tight control the security-oriented warden needed but never achieved. He offered no incentives to lure the inmates into good behavior—no reward, only punishment. Being locked up became such a common occurrence that the convicts started to use it to their own advantage. It not only tended to enhance their tough-guy image, but many looked forward to a stay in Cellblock 3. They liked the idea of finishing out their sentences in the privacy of a cell rather than in population, where violence, rape and overcrowding were increasing. Escapes continued. As one inmate explained it: "Why is someone willing to go over a fence right by a tower and risk his life, knowing that they'll shoot him if they spot him?...Because he's so frustrated with this pace—doesn't see a way out, can't work towards his freedom—that he decides it's better to be shot, it's better to be killed than to remain here."[12]

In 1978, after little more than a year on the job, Warden Malley quit in disgust. He had failed to grasp the fact that control wasn't the only way to deal with human beings. Maybe his thirty years in corrections had jaded him so thoroughly that he'd forgotten it was humanity he was dealing with. "We only stay in control of prisons to the degree that the prison population as a whole sees our administration as fair, humane, somewhat reasonable, and something they can understand. When we reach the point where a large number of prisoners see our administration as something other than that, then we have the potential for anything," commented another veteran of corrections, Lloyd Patterson, thirty years with the

California prison system. "I think most people who work in prisons...lose sight and say, 'Hey, we are in control. We got you guys, and we've got all the gas and the sticks and guns that we need to control you.' You get that idea and you're in trouble." [13]

Perhaps it was the state's recognition that a more humane administering of the prison was needed that made them appoint two gentler though less qualified men to succeed Malley. Neither the acting warden, who filled the bill while a permanent man was being sought, nor the final selection, had the experience to handle the job with authority. The highest position Warden Jerry Griffin had held in corrections before taking over the top post at Santa Fe was superintendent of the Roswell Center, a minimum security institution that included community contact and community release; hardly the background needed to run a maximum security penitentiary. In the year and a few months these two relatively weak administrators filled the role of warden, the prison fell into the full control of the Rodriguez clique once again. Deputy Warden Robert Montoya, who arrived at the institution under Warden Aaron in 1975, was now the leader, at least on the inside. The Corrections Department itself was in turmoil, having experienced as many correction secretaries as the prison had wardens. The only firm voice in the department was that of the still-powerful original kingpin, Felix Rodriguez. Many who'd worked under Rodriguez when he was warden remained at the penitentiary. Together with the deputy warden, they reinstated the power of the Santa Fe Eleven and the effective insanity of the snitch circuit.

By far the most hated member of this clique was a lieutenant nicknamed Greeneyes. Snitches weren't Greeneyes' cup of brew. His priority was playing games with an inmate's mind. He would go out of his way to make trouble for a convict, call him degrading names to his face, challenge him to talk back, and throw him in the Hole if he didn't, then get the goon squad to tear gas and beat him. I've seen him harass an inmate so many times I still have nightmares about him. Once, when I was in lockup in Cellblock 3, there was a Chicano a few cells down who knew he was getting a visit from his family that day: Greeneyes, who was on duty, had already told him to get dressed. After waiting an hour and still not being called again, the dude yelled over to Greeneyes: "Hey, you told me an hour ago to get ready, how come?"

"You better shut your mouth," Greeneyes answered, "I'm tired of hearing it. You open it again, you won't have any visiting privilege, today or any day."

What could the inmate do but sit and fume in silence. When another forty-five minutes went by, he lost his cool. The fact that he'd been told to get ready meant his visitor was already there and waiting.

"Hey, what's the delay with my visit?" he shouted again.

Greeneyes got up and called to the guard in the control booth outside the tier to come inside. When he did, the two of them walked over to the convict's cell, cranked open the door and pulled him out.

"Okay, smartass, we're taking you where you can scream all you want. You won't have to worry about your visits for a while."

When a convict is taken to the Hole, he has to wait thirty days before he's eligible to have visitors again. While he screamed and pleaded, they dragged the Chicano down to the basement, stripped him naked and shoved him into the dark maximum detention unit; all because he had the audacity to be concerned about his weekly one-hour chance to talk to someone who actually cared about him, someone who could, for sixty minutes out of his endless monotonous time, make him feel like a human being.

One day I was standing in line to get canteen supplies when Greeneyes pulled someone out of the line and made him go back to his unit without buying anything. That meant the con had to spend the week without the cigarettes, coffee, Kool-Aid and snacks that make the days go by with at least a modicum of pleasure. His great crime was that he had dropped something and stepped a few feet out of formation to pick it up. It's small things like this that build and make a man hate. Many grievances were filed against Greeneyes, but nothing ever came of them. He was, after all, a long-standing member of the Corrections clique. The administration agreed he might be a little hard on the inmates, but they backed his action and let him continue. He was so despised that during the 1980 riot the negotiators offered to give up three of their hostages if they could have Greeneyes instead.

The prison's intelligence officer was another long-time member of the clique. His job was "to collect, collate, and evaluate intelligence information affecting the safe operation of the penitentiary,"[14] and he achieved that goal by relying heavily on his snitch lines. The trouble was that he believed anything he was told and never bothered to investigate before he acted on a tip and had an inmate locked up. Consequently, grudges between inmates were often settled by channeling bogus information through this intelligence officer. Informants itching for better jobs or transfer to the honor unit knew they could feed him a lie and collect their reward. As long as it was plausible, this officer would buy it. Many a convict, innocent of the charge, has been locked up in Cellblock 3, sometimes for as long as six months, on another inmate's unproven word. I could never figure whether this so-called *intelligence* officer was stupid, lazy or thought every convict without exception was a bad-ass. Fortunately for him, two weeks before the riot he was transferred out of the penitentiary—though to another position in the Corrections Department.

Many of the guards, too, developed their own snitch lines, thereby earning for themselves the promotion given by the administration when an officer was deemed "attentive to prisoners' needs."[15] In reality, this was a power game that was dangerous, sometimes fatal, to inmates and never answered any "needs" but those of The Man's clique. When they saw a convict they wanted to turn into one of their snitches, usually a young, new inmate, a guard would approach him. At the start the kid wouldn't go for it. Then came the convincing. They'd throw him in Cellblock 5 with the hardcore cons, who'd beat and rape him. When it was all over, the captain or lieutenant would come back and offer him their protection: "You do what we need you to do and we'll keep those guys off your back." If the fish still refused, they'd put a false "snitch jacket" on him, their favorite payback to convicts they either didn't like or who wouldn't work with them. They'd let the word slip out to population that the con had been talking to them, knowing the other inmates would jump to the conclusion that it was true. Enraged as they were by their circumstances and at The Man, most convicts were happy to have some scapegoat to vent their anger on. They wouldn't sit down and figure out whether the dude really snitched on someone or if The Man was fucking with him. They'd just assume the sonofabitch had been talking. Then the guy was in trouble and fifty convicts were ready to get on his case with fists and shanks. He couldn't fight fifty men, so he had to leave population and stay locked up in the protection unit, with a reputation he hadn't earned.

Only men with basically weak constitutions, who didn't have the stamina to stand up to the punishment The Man would dish out, wound up snitching. But as much as the convicts gave the snitch a hard time, they understood that half the blame went to the upholders of the law, the so-called rehabilitators of the criminal mind, who used their positions of power to manipulate and intimidate an inmate into betraying his friends. Nor did The Man have any respect for his informers or offer them solace or reward when their usefulness was ended. Once a snitch was found out by the rest of population, it was a lonely life. If he was lucky enough to avoid getting killed, his name was forever mud. He had to spend the rest of his time locked up day and night, knowing he was despised by everyone, guards and inmates alike.

Like the snitches, Deputy Warden Montoya had the distinction of being despised by both inmates and guards. The officers would openly complain to us about him, mainly because he treated them as badly as he treated convicts. If a guard wasn't playing footsies with the clique, Montoya would give him the royal shaft by shifting him to tower duty or some equally obnoxious work detail. In some cases, Montoya made things so intolerable for the officer that he'd be forced to resign, as happened in one well-publicized incident involving a twenty-seven-year-old newcomer to the penitentiary. The way Officer Bruce Podlesny told the story, he saw a window one day with broken glass in it, "just hanging there, splintered," and knocked it out to prevent someone from cutting themselves or using the glass as a weapon. Someone, no doubt a friend of the clique, reported him for *breaking* the window, and Podlesny was called down to Montoya's office to explain. According to Podlesny, Montoya tagged him a psycho and said he didn't believe the officer had broken off already-splintered glass from just four or five panes; he believed Podlesny had actually smashed all thirty-five panes of glass in the window. Montoya gave him a choice: resign, in which case his employment record would remain clean and he wouldn't have to pay for the window, or be fired and pay for it. Podlesny resigned, but $157 was still deducted from his last paycheck, payment for the window he insisted he never broke. Montoya denied Podlesny's story, insisting that he'd never accused the officer of being a psycho or of breaking a window. "We counseled him in reference to the window breaking," he told reporters, but he didn't recall "the circumstances surrounding his termination or resignation." Nor did he know anything about the guard's final check and the deduction made on it because, he said, "my concern is programs."[16] A group of guards, however, backed up Podlesny's version of the event and used it to exemplify their own dissatisfaction with working under Montoya. "You have your little fiefdoms out there. Employees who make mistakes on the job are disciplined if they're on the outs with the power structure, but get off scot-free if they're tied to a clique."[17] They explained to the reporter that they were talking so they could get the public's attention and induce the Corrections Department to give the officers more training and more chance for advancement. Only thirty percent of the corrections staff had received formal classroom training, and even in Rodriguez's time, training to be a warden was nonexistent. Actually, by 1979 there was more formal training offered to guards than ever before, but because the prison was understaffed, few newcomers and no old-timers could be spared from duty so they could attend these classes. In addition to this formal study, new officers were supposed to receive a basic orientation during their first week on duty, but some guards reported that the program was little more than a tour of the penitentiary. "If you're lucky, a fellow officer will show you what you have to do if he has time," one guard told the Attorney General's investigators.[18] Another veteran officer told them that "his best initial instruction on key and grill handling came from inmates."[19]

The man in charge of keeping the corrections officers on their toes was another old-timer clique member. He was as lax in enforcing security procedures as he was careless in his treatment of inmates. During his seventeen years on the rise from guard to Superintendent of Correctional Security, he'd proven himself to be one of the least sympathetic officers in the penitentiary. He never took the time to talk to an inmate, regardless of the problem at hand, and if he had it would have to have been to a fellow Chicano because he could barely speak English. It was during his term as security chief that so many escapes occurred and the 1980 riot exploded. If anyone had been concerned about how the prison was being managed, they would have seen he wasn't taking care of business. Only after the riot did the laziness he allowed begin to surface. In the words of one of the officers under his command, "For sixteen hours a day and on weekends, the place was run by captains who made a lot of accommodations, causing rampant inconsistencies...At least half the time when I walked into the place in the morning...we were not flying the colors...Now, you may not be able to relate that to basic security procedures, but I do...Something is done every day all the time because it is supposed to be done."[20] Given this lack of supervision, the guards had the power to act on their own and lock up convicts for any infraction they could dream up, and they dreamed up some humdingers. Inmates were sent to lockup for walking down the wrong side of the corridor, for lying on their bunks after morning wake-up call, or for taking crackers out of the kitchen. One prisoner was sent to lockup because he'd cut his finger and smashed it while unloading trash in the dumpsite. Lockup was so prevalent a punishment there was triple bunking in Cellblock 3, while in Cellblock 4, Protection, where there should have be only one in a cell, there were two. Why? Because the snitch circuits were so carelessly used that informants were being found out as soon as they fingered someone.

None of this helped to calm the mounting rage of the inmates, nor was there any help from top management. The warden was never available to anyone and Deputy Warden Montoya was a lost cause as far as the inmates were concerned. This man was never straight with a convict. Someone would stop him and ask for a job change, or say he needed to talk to him about something important, and Montoya would say, "Sure, I'll get to you this afternoon," or "I'll call you in the morning." That would be the end of it, the inmate would never hear from him. A week later he'd see Montoya again and ask what happened to the meeting he'd promised. Montoya would look at him like he didn't know what the dude was talking about and tell him he never said any such thing. He demonstrated no interest in the wellbeing of the prisoners. His whole framework was one of force and security gained through the fear he and his officers could evoke in a man. Many of the prisoners felt that Montoya was blatantly prejudiced against whites and blacks, especially those who belonged to the cliques. Inmates believed that he would lock up members of the Aryan Brotherhood on the slightest provocation, and they felt that he had even less use for the Black Muslims, while it seemed he'd bend over backwards for his brother Chicanos. When six Chicanos jumped one white inmate, beating and raping him, and the white con turned them in, Montoya had no choice but to lock the Chicanos up. The next day, though, he gave them more slack than he'd ever given a white or black. He called them into his office and asked if they'd done what they were accused of. Naturally they said no. "Six against one, that's good enough for me," Montoya told them. "I can't see any reason to hold you guys in lockup any more." They were freed from lockup in just one day. A few months later, however, he had no qualms about holding a group of whites and one black in lockup for weeks, in spite of a report from one of his own officers that there were no grounds to do so.

There were other actions of Montoya's that triggered the February riot, in particular one that centered on mail and visitation. A few jailhouse lawyers had filed lawsuits to secure improvements in certain prison conditions. After waiting two and a half years for the courts to take action on this suit, the Duran Decree, a "partial consent decree" was signed in the fall of 1979. It ordered the implementation of increased mail and visitation privileges, privileges that in the joint are life-breath to an inmate. When the court order came through, Montoya took his mean, slow, time instituting these new policies. This infuriated the convicts, many of whom were clique leaders who'd worked hard and waited a long time to see the fruits of their efforts.[20a]

Another trigger that made the prison blow apart was the insidious work going on in the psychological services unit. Dr. Mark Orner, the psychologist heading the unit, was also a member of The Man's clique. His actions during his time at the penitentiary had earned him the animosity of the inmates, which they expressed during the riot by burning down the psych unit with particular vigor. As a former inmate told reporters, "The overkill and butchery you saw during the riot was one of rage, and the rage was from the stress in that prison. And it's my opinion that the psychological services unit added to that stress more than it reduced the rage."[21] Like the other clique members, Dr. Orner played one inmate off against the other. In addition, his evaluations of a convict had a great amount of pull with the parole board, and he used that fact to gather information: if a man didn't tell him what he wanted to know, Orner would tell the board the con wasn't ready for society yet. Since, as a psychologist, he was thought to have a special talent for understanding human nature, the board went along with his opinion ninety-nine percent of the time. The psychological services unit was started in 1973. Most of the convicts thought it was a big joke and a waste of money. They had no respect for Orner from the gitgo, and as time went on, no trust in him or his counselors. They knew Orner's staff reported back to him, and they weren't about to unburden their feelings so he could ruin their records if he didn't like what he heard. When new inmates would mistakenly go to the counselors for help in handling the jungle they were facing for the first time, the advice they were given was the same they would have gotten from a guard or administrator: Go on back and tough it out. Even if Orner and his staff had been willing to honestly work with the problems a man faces in the penitentiary, where would they begin? Convicts aren't about to unload to The Man when their entire day-to-day existence deals in secret plots to get around the administration; nor are they likely to confide in a psychologist who was a member of the punishment-dealing segregation committee, as Orner was.

The psychological problems in prison can't be solved by talking about them anyway. It's prison itself that breeds paranoia, depression, and aggressive feelings. Dr. Orner was only a doctor of psychology. Though he denied it, reports always managed to circulate that he was strongly opposed to the hiring of a psychiatrist. When a team of forensic health care consultants for the American Civil Liberties Union came to the penitentiary in 1979 to inspect the medical facilities, a psychiatrist in the group quoted Dr. Orner as telling him, "'I'll leave if a psychiatrist comes here'...Orner told me that he had spent seven years building up his psychological services staff and that he did not want any outsiders threatening his position or his staff's credibility."[22] According to this team of consultants, Dr. Orner and his psychological services unit never supplied adequate care for the mentally ill, who made up ten percent of the prison population. Because these psychotic inmates were thrown into dormitories with the mainstream of convicts, they were cause or victim of "nearly half the violent incidents within the penitentiary"[23] and usually would end up in the Hole for indefinite periods of time without the benefit of the therapy or tranquilizers their condition demanded. What little counseling they did receive consisted of one of Orner's aids walking by their windowless cell door asking a brief, "How's everything today?" Dr. Orner and the prison's medical director both had "antipathy to psychiatry, psychiatrists and the use of psychotropic medication, including major tranquilizers,"[24] the latter being standard treatment for psychotic and schizophrenic disorders. The forensic unit of the state hospital in Las Vegas, New Mexico, where these mentally ill convicts should and would have gone were it not so overcrowded, wrote to this team of medical consultants that "prisoners arrive from the penitentiary in a catatonic state and it is obvious they are receiving no treatment."[25] They cited as example one prisoner who was considered "a raving lunatic" and transferred to Las Vegas. Through the use of Loxitane, an antipsychotic, he reached what doctors described as a "stable remission," stable enough for him to be sent back to the penitentiary. When he returned there, he was given no medication, even though it had been prescribed, and "soon became floridly psychotic again."[26]

Some of those inmates whose mental balance went awry managed to escape their suffering by killing themselves. Between 1968 and 1977, there were seven successful suicides in the prison, and in the following year, between June 1978 and May 1979, several more suicide attempts were recorded. Those who tried but didn't succeed were placed in lockup or in a special dungeon Hole near the gas chamber in the basement of Cellblock 5, where no guards were stationed and no one could hear their constant screams to be set free. Others who were more violently suicidal were treated to one of the most bizarre procedures in prison history, a plaster body cast from neck to ankles, with holes for defecation and urination. This restraint was developed in 1978 by the penitentiary's medical director as an alternative to drug therapy. As he explained to the team of forensic consultants, he thought it was "probably more humane to physically restrain people"[27] than to make them suffer the affects of some tranquilizers. His premise is voided by the fact that Thorazine had to be forced down a fit-throwing convict's throat to get him into the body cast. Dr. Orner spoke about his use of these casts at a meeting of the American Medical Association's Conference on Health Services in Correctional Facilities in November of 1979. He told his audience that he was using body casts as a method of crisis intervention. "And he did it in almost a bragging tone—he sounded like he thought it was terrific," one listener, an attorney with the New York Legal Aid Society, commented. "I asked him how he got people into it, considering that they would be supposedly violent people in some kind of episode, and he said that if it took six officers, eight officers, it didn't matter how many it took to hold the guy down."[28] But according to an interview with an ex-inmate who was placed in a body cast in the summer of 1979, it was Thorazine, not guards, that subdued him:

I was brought down to the hospital in handcuffs, and thrown off into the strip cell a number of times. Finally they upped and stuffed me off in that ol' cast situation…But before they did that, they poured Thorazine down my throat. Held my jaws right there, and just poured it right in my face because I didn't want to take it. Well…after I got in that full body cast, I busted all out of that, man, because I was hysterical. Scared. Somebody's trying to kill me…"[29]

A psychologist from an east coast mental health unit, who treated this man before he'd gone into the Land of Enchantment's prison, told reporters he "seriously deteriorated while in the New Mexico state pen. He came back much worse than when he went out there. He returned totally schizophrenic."[30]

Punishment was the prison's going treatment for insanity. When a psychotic, mentally disturbed convict was brought before the segregation committee, which included psychologist Mark Orner, the man would be treated like he'd done something wrong, sent to lockup or stripped naked and thrown in the Hole or, worse yet, the Dungeon Hole near the gas chamber. All his privileges were taken away—no canteen, no visits, no television. Five of the inmates killed in the February 1980 riot were mentally ill. One was Juan Sanchez, who died in the Hole. Two were in the protection unit, Cellblock 4, one in Cellblock 3, and the other was new enough to the prison to still be living in population. They were killed because none of the prisoners understood their insanity any more than the administration did. "Do you know why it's so hard to treat the mentally disturbed prisoners at the state pen?" a former New Mexico prison psychologist asked rhetorically, then aptly answered: "Because it's the institution that has a character disorder."[31]

# 7

*The dude that sent me to the penitentiary for life, someone who's sittin' over there doin' six months while I'm sittin' here doin' life and I got a chance to get to that dude? You bet I'm gonna break my back to get to him. The guy they burned all to pieces with a cuttin' torch, well he deserved that a hundred times more. Whoever did that ought to get a medal pinned on his chest. A baby raper and a child molester, that's a sick individual and he's got anything comin' that anybody does to him.*

—Inmate, Penitentiary of New Mexico[1]

## 5:00 A.M., Saturday, February 2, 1980.

The fire in the psychological services unit was roaring. Rioters had turned the blowtorch to the unit to put the finishing touch on its destruction. Just above it, in the old men's dormitory where I was, the smoke was getting so thick we began to think we wouldn't get out alive. Flames were licking up the stairwell, the only exit, and the intense heat from the fire below made it impossible to stand on the floor. Finally someone remembered that the band practice room was just behind our dormitory. Using the metal beds as battering rams, we managed to knock through a wall into the room and save our lives. There were windows there which we smashed open, each of us stationing ourselves by a broken pane and breathing in fresh air.

The band room overlooked the front gate of the penitentiary. We could see that police had already arrived, and over the two-way radio a rioter had given us we'd been hearing that Deputy Warden Montoya was there also. We tried to contact him, but it took a while.

"The smoke is real bad up here," we told him when we finally got him on the two-way. "It's beginning to get to a lot of men. The fire's so hot downstairs it looks like the floor might collapse, and if it does, there's fifty or sixty men here that will burn to death."

"There's nothing we can do to help you," Montoya answered. "None of the administration is coming into the penitentiary. The only thing you can do is find some way out on your own."

"But we *can't* get out. The only way out is blocked by flames and smoke, no one can get through."

Someone who thought they could get the point across better grabbed the radio. "Man, we're burnin' up. You gotta do something or everyone up here's gonna be cremated; can't you bring us some chains at least, so we can jerk these windows loose and jump out?"

"That's your problem," was the deputy warden's reply. "You'll have to get out the best way you can." End of communication.

Fortunately, some of the blacks next door in Cellhouse 6 were interested in using the band room as a command post and decided to help us. They broke the emergency glass that encased a fire hose in the hallway, took the hose and hooked it up to a faucet in the janitorial closet between the two units and drenched the stairway. When the flames were subdued, rioters wearing gas masks made their way upstairs through the smoke to see what they could do for us. They offered the masks to anyone who wanted to go down to the gymnasium, but there were no takers. By this time the open windows and the dousing of the fire had cleared the air somewhat and we decided, again, not to leave. Aside from our wariness about the sanity of the rioters, there were a few in the old-men's dorm who were guilty of sex crimes and feared they might be harmed if recognized by some drugged, raving con.

The blacks set up their command post in the band room, with its full-on view of the front of the prison and the activities of the police. They had several two-way radios, and, to distract ourselves from the smoke and heat we paid attention to the transmissions between the riot negotiators and The Man outside. From these we learned that the rioters had taken a blowtorch to the grill that blocked the Protection Unit and the empty Cellblock 5 from the main corridor.

"Hey, *ese*," the Chicano voice said to someone calling himself Chopper One. "We're just now starting to cut the grill. When we get through, we're gonna burn into 5 and see if there are any more torches in there, or whatever else we can use when we get into Protection. We're goin' down after the snitches, gonna kill us some of those motherfuckers, man."

"Okay," Chopper One answered. "You get it open, you let me know. I wanna get that snitchin' bastard that sent me into lockup for six months, send him home to his mama."

For the next hour and a half we heard them talking back and forth about their progress.

"Well, how're you doin'?" Chopper One called to ask at one point. "How long is it gonna take you guys to get those bars cut?"

"Well, we're still at it; I think we're runnin' low on oxygen. Someone will have to go down and get another bottle."

Deputy Warden Montoya and his crew outside were also picking up these transmissions and knew that a massacre of snitches was imminent. They knew, too, that it was going to take the rioters some time to cut through the two sets of bars; time enough for police to come in by the sally-port area in the rear of the prison, enter Cellblock 4 by a back entrance—to which they were supposed to have keys in the front guard tower—and lead the ninety-six men in the snitch unit out to safety. Even if they didn't have the keys to the back door, there was a garage in the sally-port area where other cutting torches were kept. They could have attempted what the rioters were doing and cut the doors open. But they didn't. Later, prison administrators would explain to investigators that the set of keys in the tower was incomplete: there were keys to the back door of the cellblock but none to the grill allowing entrance into the cell area. Whether it was a matter of missing keys or missing motivation is a question that will be debated for years, both privately and in courts hearing the claims of families whose sons, brothers and husbands were killed due in great part to the negligence of prison authorities.

The deputy warden and superintendent of correctional security had arrived at the main gatehouse in front of the prison shortly after the riot began; easy to do because they both lived on the penitentiary grounds. Warden Jerry Griffin also lived on the grounds, and joined them a few minutes later. As one of his first tactics, the security chief armed the tower officers with riot guns and instructed them to fire on anyone attempting to escape. This proved an unnecessary move. The inmates made it clear in their first radio communication with these officials that they weren't going to try to escape, they were holding out for a meeting with the news media and Governor Bruce King. But the rioters warned that if the National Guard or state police tried to rush the institution, they would kill their hostages. They put the dog-leashed and beaten Captain Roybal on the radio to confirm their intentions.

The three administrators talked it over and agreed to negotiate the release of the hostages rather than attempt to retake the penitentiary. By common consent, Montoya was designated negotiator. He'd recently returned from San Francisco, where he'd taken a timely course in crisis intervention and hostage situations. His strategy was to keep the rioters from talking to the Governor and the warden. Setting up first in his car and then in the gatehouse, Montoya used a handset radio to carry on his talks with the inmate negotiators. He conducted himself in the manner learned at "hostage school,"[2] alternating between soothing and harsh tones. Most of his dialogues were with Chopper One, but the person behind that name changed several times throughout the negotiations. So many inmates had two-way radios that it was hard to decipher what was being said or who was really in the position to speak for the rioters. Montoya's radio was also picking up communications from sheriff's officers who had arrived on the scene, so that many inmate transmissions were lost in the confusion. He finally demanded that the sheriffs stop using the radios, and the babble calmed enough for him to hear Chopper One's demands. It became clear that regardless of the change in person behind the name, Chopper One was the main negotiation station. Most inmate demands made during these early hours remained consistent throughout the uprising. The prison was not to be rushed or the hostages would be killed. They wanted to talk with the Governor, the warden, Deputy Secretary of Corrections Felix Rodriguez, and the news media. They wanted a public forum to air their complaints about "poor food, overcrowding, mismanagement at the penitentiary, and inadequate recreation."[3] And they asked for the resignation of the administrators they most despised: Deputy Warden Montoya himself, Associate Warden Adelaido Martinez; the Superintendent of Correctional Security, Manuel Koroneos, and Lieutenant Benito Gonzales, known better by inmates as Greeneyes.

It wasn't until Felix Rodriguez arrived that action on the convicts' behalf began. A hose was dragged to the main entrance of the prison to try and combat the fires, though it did little good. Wounded prisoners were allowed to be brought out for treatment. This netted a reward for the administration. The helpful inmates who'd hidden Officer Herman Gallegos in a dormitory at the start of the riot smuggled him past rioters and through the main entrance by dressing him in a prison uniform and arming him with a pipe. Rodriguez was fair but firm. He demanded to know how many hostages were being held and their names.

Riot negotiators were also firm. They fired back over the radio: "If you don't start negotiating pretty soon, these guards are going to get wasted, Captain Roybal will be the first one to pop out of the door dead."

Rodriguez countered that if there were no assurances the hostages were still alive he would order the SWAT team inside the penitentiary. "And if that happens," he said, "it's going to be worse than Attica. Kill one of my officers and we'll come in and kill every one of you."

By then the entire penitentiary had been surrounded by state police, sheriff's officers and the Santa Fe SWAT team. The Governor had been notified of the riot, and the National Guard was on its way. Meanwhile everyone's radio sets were buzzing with transmissions about the progress of those torching through the grill to Cellblock 4 and threats against the snitches' lives.

"All them guys in Cellblock 4 that you've been using," someone broadcast directly to Deputy Warden Montoya, "well, I've got some of them in the sack just in case you don't cooperate. Eyewitnesses, that you call the snitches...they're all gonna get shanked."[4] That the killing of the inmates in Cellblock 4 would occur, these administrators had no doubt. They knew the hardcore men in Cell-block 3 had been released, they'd seen them moving up and down the hallways through the windows. But Montoya's newly learned hostage strategy held: no police or staff members were to go near the prison. The major objective was to keep the hostages from being killed. If ninety-six convicts faced being burned to death because of that strategy, it clearly was of no consequence, and an extension of the public's attitude toward a person convicted of committing a crime.

### 7:00 A.M., daybreak, Groundhog Day.

Through the billowing smoke that shaded the sunrise, the guard staffing the south tower spotted an inmate crawling out of a window in Unit E, waving a white towel. The men in E-1, the semi-protection unit, had managed to forge an opening in a window with the pipe wrench Joe Madrid died providing them. When the sirens screaming through the front gates of the penitentiary stopped, the tower guard could hear the man shouting, "We want to surrender, we want to surrender."

The officer cocked his gun and aimed it at the convict before he leaned out of the tower window and yelled back: "Okay, come out with your hands on top of your head and lay down on your stomach."

The inmate did as he was told. The guard used his bullhorn to address the men still inside the dormitory.

"Come out one at a time, with your hands on your head, and get down on your stomachs."

The window opening was big enough for only one man at a time anyway. In twenty minutes, though, all eighty-seven residents of the semi-protection unit had crawled through it and were lying face down on the cold ground outside. They were the first of hundreds of convicts who would run from the insanity inside the prison during the next thirty hours.

The inmates in the full Protection Unit, Cellblock 4, the snitch cage, didn't have such luck. As the men in E-1 found freedom, the rioters wielding the cut-ting torch succeeded in melting through the last hinge of the protection unit grill. Thirty minutes before, they'd gotten into Cellblock 5, which was undergoing renovation, and found two more acetylene torches. They'd been left by the construction crew—even though, two weeks after the December escape of eleven inmates, a memo had been sent to the superintendent of security by two guards suggesting that these tools be removed from the institution each day. Later the security chief would say he never saw that memo. These torches now became instruments of torture. Wearing bandanas pulled up over their faces and ski hats pulled over their hair the rioters ran through the opened grill up and down the catwalks of each tier, yelling, "We're comin' after you bastards, we're gonna kill you sorryass motherfuckers." They were specific about who they wanted, however. They went straight for the guard station where the picture roster of everyone in the cellblock was kept. Once they found the cell numbers of the men they were targeting, they divided into groups, roaming the three tiers until they found them. Getting their marks out of the cell wasn't so easy.

When they realized the door to the cellblock was being torched, those in the unit who thought there was a good chance they'd be on the most wanted list had begun taking security measures. They made smoke bombs of their mattresses, tearing them open, stuffing them with toilet paper, and setting them on fire, hoping that when the rioters broke into the catwalk it would be so thick with smoke they'd be forced out or at least slowed down until help could be gotten. The rioters weren't slowed, and help never came. The men in Protection prepared for that eventuality, too. Lifting their beds on end, they had jammed the legs into the door rail to keep it from being cranked open and tied bed sheets around the door and bars of the cell to further insure their safety. Then they armed themselves with chair and table legs and waited for the onslaught.

While bands of masked inmates went looking for the objects of their wrath, taking blowtorches to cut through the barricaded doors, others freed their friends. The black contingent was particularly anxious to get the Black Muslim minister out before the bloodshed began. Because so many inmates had jammed their doors, the lever on the main control board that released the locking device to his cell was stuck. Since his friends couldn't therefore merely crank his door open, they had to get one of the cutting torches and burn through the hinges. When he was free, he immediately cautioned the rioters not to harass the blacks in the unit; he was going to take them out with him. Whites and Chicanos agreed. Though the Aryan Brotherhood's threats on the black leader's life had caused the administration to place the Muslim in Protection, the whites wanted no trouble with him now. In fact, they were anxious to have the power of his group with them and gave him no hassle as he went about releasing all the blacks in the cellblock—al but one, a paranoid schizophrenic named Paulina Paul, who the Muslim minister thought would be safer in his cell than roaming among the berserk convicts. Once all the blacks were out of their cells, the Muslim minister took them to Cellhouse 6, where his people were headquartered. When he got there, he was immediately given a rundown of what had occurred thus far in the riot. A Chicano contingent came to see him a few minutes later and asked him to be the spokesman for the blacks in the riot. The minister had heard and seen enough, however, to be sure of his answer. Between the torture of Archie Martinez and the free flow of drugs, he could read the handwriting on the wall. He was an educated, religious man, and the trend of this uprising offended his sensibilities.

"This isn't for us," the minister told them. "We don't want anything to do with it. We won't interfere with you, but we won't participate either."

Reluctantly the Chicanos accepted his decision and left. But the blacks knew they'd taken a dangerous position. The Muslim leader's first plan of action was to look for a way out of the prison before the rioters decided to off them as traitors.

Back in Cellblock 4, five Chicanos were looking for their friend, an ace lieutenant in their clique and one of the most criminally insane men in the institution, a convict who'd raped his own wife with a hot curling iron (the very same inmate my P.O. said I was just like). Once his men freed him, he armed himself with a butcher knife, provided by a bro, and became a leading figure on the death squad that had already begun doling out retribution to chosen snitches. The dozen or so men who made up the squad—members of the Aryan Brotherhood, the Mexican Mafia, and a few unaffiliated blacks—broke up into small bands and roamed the three floors of the cellblock, opening the jammed cell doors with the flames of cutting torches, verbally gnawing on the mind of the victim trapped inside, describing in gory detail the tortures they would subject him to once the door was opened.

Up on the top tier, a large black executioner, wielding a mean knife, stood alone in front of the cell of the prison's number one snitch.

"Aha, sucker, I got you by the balls now," he announced, hacking away at the sheets that were wrapped around the bars of the door and cell. But the informer was a survivor.

"The fuck you do," he answered, unshaken by the confrontation. He'd not only jammed his door with the bed, he'd armed himself with a club-like chair leg. Every time the executioner put his hand out to whack away the sheets, the snitch slammed it with the weapon. Soon the black man saw he was getting nowhere and stopped.

"I'll be back, cocksucker, with a cuttin' torch to burn you out of there, then we'll see how fuckin' tough you are."

When his tormenter was gone, the informer seized on the first opportunity to get himself out of there. A Chicano himself, he pleaded with the first homeboy to pass by his cell and got lucky. The man he chose was a newcomer and didn't recognize the snitch as anyone but an ethnic brother. The fish went to the office where the mechanism controlling the locking of the cells was and flipped the switch to the informant's door. Quickly the snitch scurried out and down the catwalk, bandana pulled over his face, ski cap on his head, and a prison-issued jacket covering the overalls with SEG stamped on the back. He looked like the rest of the rioters rushing through the cellblock. Others were also escaping the Protection Unit this way.

"Hey, open up my cell door so I can get out and kill me some people," they'd yell to the cons passing their cells. If they weren't on the hit list or weren't recognized, their doors would be unlocked. All but twelve men in the cellblock were set free eventually. The execution squad was selective; there was an ethic to their madness, though that didn't stop them from giving Protection residents a harrowing time before they were released, making them wonder whether their number was up. Those lucky enough to get out of their cells had no way of knowing that the rioters were being choosy about who they killed. Swiftly they suited up to look like the rest of the rioters, grabbed weapons and made their way out of the unit, either to participate in destruction in other parts of the prison or to find a hiding place.

The number-one snitch who managed to escape before his black tormenter could return had the sense to know he could not take his chances mingling, and sought a hiding place. He was on the top tier of Cellblock 3 looking up at the ceiling, trying to find the fine crack that would tell him a portion of the plasterboard had been cut open to stash someone's home brew or weapons in. He knew he could fit in the two-foot crawl space between the board and the real ceiling. But he was caught off guard by another Chicano who recognized him and stuck a teargas gun in his back, then marched him downstairs to the basement of Cellblock 3. Luck was still with the informer though. In the process of the journey, his captor ran into some friends and stopped to talk to them. The snitch instantly took advantage of the moment and, aided by the thick smoke that filled the corridor and hampered visibility, ran to the basement tier of the hospital. There he found a fellow informer who'd cut his own hiding place in the false ceiling and was happy to share it. The two remained there for the entire riot, probably offering many thanks to their god as they listened to the agonized screams of their brother snitches whose luck had run out.

Those screams wailed through all the cellblocks on the north side. The guard held hostage there had to be having nightmare visions of the torture causing them and the specter of being the next victim. Captain Roybal, who had already been through a brutal ordeal as one of the first guards captured, suffered a mild heart attack. Whatever he'd imagined, it came nowhere near the demonic reality that had taken over in Cellblock 4. Some were killed the easy way, cremated to death by gasoline or paint thinner thrown into their cells along with a lit match or the flames of the torch. Others paid the hard way. One man was held down, convulsing as his executioners hammered a metal rod through his head. When they stopped, the man was dead; blood soaked his face and the hands and clothes of his killers, and the rod stuck out of the other side of his skull. Across the way on the other side of the tier, a group led by a member of the Aryan Brotherhood approached the cell of a white man who I'll call Bear. The leader recognized Bear not as a snitch but a sniveler who'd gone to The Man and asked to be locked up because he couldn't pay a gambling debt to someone in the brotherhood. Bear hadn't jammed his cell door and now, while one of the death squad was walking to the control center to unlock it, he used the wit he'd planned to count on and begged for his life.

"Please, give me a break, you know I'm a bro, I'll do anything you say," he told him.

The biker thought it over for a second, then, with a malicious grin, answered, "Okay, we'll give you a chance. If you kill the nigger in the cell next to you, we'll let you live."

Bear swallowed hard as his door slid open. He wasn't a killer. He'd made his deal, though, and for his own life's sake he agreed to the initiation. The "nigger" he was to murder was Paulina Paul, the paranoid schizophrenic the Black Muslim minister had left in the cell for safety's sake.

Paulina Paul was one of the penitentiary's ten percent who'd been diagnosed as mentally ill. He'd been regarded as crazy even in childhood, and considering the name his parents cursed him with, it's no wonder. Imagine growing up as a stud in a black neighborhood with the name of a girl! Criminal insanity ran in Paulina Paul's family. His brother went berserk in a Viet Nam movie theater, fatally shooting five fellow American soldiers and wounding four others. Another brother shot a cop in Albuquerque; and his sister killed her three-year-old child.5 Compared to their deeds, Paulina Paul's armed robbery of a hotel in Alamogordo, New Mexico, was peanuts. His actions during his trial, however, were not. He had to be tied to his chair to keep him in the courtroom, which didn't stop him from bombarding judge and jury with "loud, animal-type noises" and "religious chants."[6] Nevertheless, he was convicted as if he were sane. He was first sent to the mental hospital in Las Vegas, New Mexico, until they deemed him fit to serve his sentence in Santa Fe. Even Dr. Orner knew Paulina Paul wasn't sane enough to withstand population. Convicts are notorious for their lack of tolerance toward mental illness. Paulina was sent to lockup in Cellblock 3, where he could be by himself and loll about naked on the cold cement floor, one of his favorite pastimes.[7]

Paulina Paul was to experience a death that matched the insanity of his thirty-six years. As his cell door was opened, Bear ran inside and plunged a butcher knife into Paulina's stomach. It wasn't a fatal puncture, however. Paulina staggered out onto the tier, clutching the wound and howling in pain.

"Here, let me show you how it's done," the lead executioner said, and took the knife from Bear. He grabbed Paulina by his hair and jerked him to the floor. While the other four on this execution squad held the squirming black man down, the biker first hacked then sawed through his neck, muttering curses about niggers and insanity while he tenaciously severed skin, bone, and muscle, until Paulina Paul's head rolled off his body. He had the distinction of being the only black man killed in the riot.

Meanwhile another group of executioners on the second tier of the cellblock had just burned a cell door off its hinges. They dragged the terrified occupant out, tied him spread-eagle to the bars and started beating him with pipes and riot batons. His screams of "please don't kill me, let me live, I want to go home, I want to see my mother, I want to see my wife just one more time" only brought sadistic laughter and renewed vigor to the beating. They didn't let up until the man lapsed into unconsciousness. Then they untied him and threw him over the catwalk railing. They watched him fall all the way down until he landed back first on the ground floor, his legs twitching in a final throe of agonized life. At the same time, three men on the floor above had bashed an inmate's head against the wall, slipped a rope around his neck and hung him from the railing, where his corpse dangled until a band of rioters not involved in the killing cut it down.

There were many small groups of executioners at this point in the riot, and they were ferociously slashing open stomachs, cutting off genitalia, beating on the corpses that were strewn over the catwalks. The floors were covered with clotted pools of blood, the cells with bloody drag marks, the air with the cries and smells of men being tortured and burned. Executioners and scavengers alike were so inundated with barbiturates they hardly saw or heard the horror they were producing. To them it was one more day in the jungle, but this day they were free to be the predators. The death dealers felt no guilt. They were acting on the strict prison ethic of payback. They were in their heyday, working off months and years of pent-up rage by gouging out eyes and pounding on bloated bodies. When a group of them found Paulina Paul's decapitated head, they stuck it on top of a broomstick and paraded around the prison with it in a primitive rite of victory. They had the decency to eventually return it to Paulina's body, where it remained until the riot approached its end. Then convict negotiators brought the corpse outside the building with the head stuck between its legs, a warning to officials of what would happen if inmates' demands were not met.

Maybe they would have struck more fear in the officials' hearts if they'd brought out the charred remains of the two men tortured to death with the pressured flames of acetylene torches. One, an informant, was held down by four of the executioners while a fifth turned the torch straight into his eyes, burning them until the back of his head exploded from the pressure and heat. Those who found his body later could still see the terror on what was left of his face. This murder was seen by a prison secretary who was watching through binoculars from the perimeter fence outside the penitentiary. "I heard some whistling and I looked over toward the cells and they just had a torch and were burning somebody's head," she told news people afterwards. "He was screaming. I couldn't believe it. It was like a nightmare."

The worst nightmare in the cellblock, however, was the execution of thirty-four-year-old James Perrin. The death squad saved him for last. Perrin was serving a life sentence for raping and murdering two little girls and their mother. In every prison in the nation, baby rapers ("short eyes") are despised, the one criminal in the jungle worse than all the others, someone even the most deranged convict can look down on. Everyone, after all, especially when insecure and oppressed, needs someone they can feel superior to. Jimmy Perrin had barricaded himself in his cell, thanks to the advice of his next-door neighbor, who'd been like a brother to him since moving to the adjacent cell a year before. Perrin's friend had instructed him in the ways and means of protecting himself, knowing he'd be a sure target for death. By the time the rioters broke into the unit, Perrin's fear had thrown him into shock. When one of the executioners stood in front of his cell, taunting him with threats of death and mutilation, Perrin stood mute and glassy-eyed behind his bed, leaning his full three hundred pounds against it to keep the legs jamming the door. All the torches were in use at the time, so the executioner had to put off his plans for the baby raper.

"I'll be back to cut you out of there later, man," the executioner promised, and went on his way.

When Perrin's friend was freed by other residents of the cellblock, he tried to convince the baby raper to take the barricade down and come out with him, but James Perrin had slipped into catatonia. All he could do was stand in the back of the upraised bed, pushing it rhythmically as if he were a dog humping a table leg, looking like his mind had gone. That was the last his friend saw of him. When he came back to the Cellblock thirty minutes later to try and talk James out of the cell again, he didn't even bother going inside. He heard Perrin's screams and knew it was too late.

Like most criminals, James Perrin's undoing was a lack of love and education, deficiencies that caused intense emotional instability when triggered by the normal heartbreaks of living. James Perrin wasn't proud of the crime he'd committed, as he expressed in a letter to a woman whose friendship he tried to cultivate four months before he died:

> First let me say that you might of heard of me. I was known as one of the Chaparrel killers. I was born in Deming, New Mexico, and then when I was twenty-two moved to El Paso, Texas, with my wife. We got a divorce in 1977 and I started going to pieces. On the street I push eighteen wheels around the countryside for a living. Yes, I make good money. And that's what causes my trouble in my marriage. I work too hard for a good living for them and she didn't care for that or me. Now I am here, I was running from state to state picking up work here and there and just living in my truck, until I came back to El Paso to see my sister. And now this thing happens to me. Now I look back and see myself, and the truth is so ugly to take. You see, I am thirty-three years old and I have nobody to really call a friend. I would like to write and carry on a correspondence with somebody and especially of the opposite sex. I just want to be liked and loved by someone who cares.

There would be no caring for Jimmy Perrin in this life. After blowtorching his door open, four executioners, including the one who'd originally taunted him, dragged James out of his cell, tied him spread-eagle to the bars and cooked him slowly with the roaring flame of the acetylene torch, melting his three hundred pounds of flesh to bone. They worked on him for half an hour, first burning his genitals, then his face, moving the torch up and down his body, bringing him around with smelling salts when he drifted into the comfort of unconsciousness, until nothing could bring him back anymore. Maybe this was enough penance to save Jimmy Perrin from any future hells.

# 8

*The prison system, inherently unjust and inhumane, is the ultimate expression of injustice and inhumanity in the society at large. Those of us on the outside do not like to think of wardens and guards as our surrogates. Yet they are, and they are intimately locked in a deadly embrace with their human captives behind the prison walls. By extension so are we. A terrible double meaning is thus imparted to the original question of human ethics: am I my brothers' keeper?*

—Jessica Mitford[1]

When I came in, the Penitentiary of New Mexico was only six years old. It had been built because the situation at the old prison had become so explosive the legislature could no longer avoid the issue. Brick and mortar do not a change make, however. The same conditions that forced the closing of the old facility continues. All the state had bought itself was a newer, larger animal house.

The situation had been intolerable for five years before the legislature even decided to investigate the old institution, no less make any changes. It's the same old problem that has existed since the beginning of penal institutions: the public doesn't want to know about them. They don't want to think about what makes a human being become a so-called criminal any more than they want to know how he's treated once he's been arrested. They're content to hide him away in a remote fortress: out of sight, out of mind. But America is finding out that this old adage no longer holds true when it comes to the treatment of its criminal element. People are discovering that it's the penitentiaries themselves that are keeping the crime rate up. Most convicts are going to be back on the streets after they've served their sentences, and as things are, they're going to be filled with the hate and rage prison life incites. The fact is, U.S. prisons are not only hate factories, they're crime factories. But as long as John Q. Public refuses to look the problem in the eye, neither will their senators and representatives, who *could* initiate change. It has proven true, at least to convicts, that legislators act only when inmates take the matter into their own hands and cause a disturbance big enough to attract the public's attention. In the mind of a convict, a riot is a legitimate means of communication. In December 1948, the residents of the old Penitentiary of New Mexico rioted in protest over the bad food and the steward in charge of cooking it. Six months later, a fight between two prisoners stirred other inmates to express their frustrations in a violent disturbance in the prison yard.

In November 1950 another riot erupted over a "feud between prisoners and guards,"[2] as the legislative committee report gently termed it; though a number of guards were injured.

There was an unsuccessful escape attempt in June 1952 that caused a guard to be killed and the warden to resign. Six months hence there was another escape attempt, with the escapees forcing open a vault and confiscating the guns stored inside it. These convicts were subdued before they could get away or use the weapons. But tensions in the prison didn't ease up. The next month there was a fight between rival gangs that left one inmate stabbed to death and several others wounded.

Even after these four years of chronic violent eruptions, New Mexico's legislature didn't take immediate action. It took yet another uprising by inmates to make the public insist that their government representatives do something about the penitentiary. Crime is a politically dangerous subject, so politicians don't usually take a stand on it until their constituency pushes them to do so. Former Governor Jerry Apodaca summed this up in explaining why his efforts to reform the penitentiary failed: "Who cares about the penitentiary? Inmates? Well, how many are there, twelve hundred, maybe thirteen hundred at the highest? They can't even vote; they're a very small constituency. Sure, they have families, they have friends, but sometimes the local pressures from society are much greater."[3] In 1953, the Legislature at last assigned a committee to investigate the causes of violence in the state's prison. The expert they brought in to head this inquiry was Douglas C. Rigg, former assistant warden at San Quentin. Rigg's report blamed the institution's problems on factors that have existed in prisons since their inception and continue to exist in these "enlightened" times: "…an inadequate system of classifying inmates for placement and security…idleness, lack of education and recreation, insufficient medical services, untrained and underpaid guards, and little dissemination of information to the press and public."[4] Rigg told the legislative committee that "the incidents of violence are actually symptoms and not causes of bad conditions. The conditions outlined in my report took years to develop. I believe my recommendations will help improve them. *In the last analysis, the prison conditions are the responsibility of the legislature, which expresses the will of the people.*"[5]

The will of the people of New Mexico was to apply brick and mortar to the situation, plus a dollop of good intentions to pave the road to the future. The new Penitentiary of New Mexico—twenty-four years later to become site of the most savage prison riot in America's history—opened on April 20, 1956, with the usual ribbon-cutting ceremony and public relations hype. Touting it as a model of humane corrections, the state handed out a press release listing "fifty brief facts and figures about the institution,"[6] citing the million gallons of water the pumps could move each day, the 132,000 bags of cement used to construct the facility, and the $24,000 spent on the gas chamber. The release ended with a brief statement of political rhetoric: "Walls and bars make a prison, but they don't change men for the better. Our objective, through group and individual training, is to try to discharge these men to the free community as law-abiding, responsible citizens who can and will support themselves and their dependents."[7] But by 1958, Warden H.R. Swenson was reporting to the legislature that "the major problem facing the penitentiary now is prisoner idleness. If all the jobs were counted up, there would be work for about three hundred men...although New Mexico has one of the finest penal institutions in the country, it could be destroyed in a year if the men are not kept occupied."[8] As well and as usual there was the problem of prison personnel. "Of greatest importance...is the selection, training, and proper utilization of personnel," Warden Swenson said. "The old concept of the officer who is only a guard is giving way to the recognition that he is actually a supervisor and as such has responsibilities requiring qualifications, training, and compensation beyond those required for purely security work."[9] Again, however, the politicians didn't listen. It was only an opinion, and their constituents didn't seem to share, or care about, it. The legislature was willing to provide money for literally concrete changes, but not for the people inside the concrete, not in terms of rehabilitation programs or in raises for corrections officers.

In 1956, a guard's starting salary was $265 a month. A stenographer in a secretarial pool was making as much. This was of course not enough money to attract a man with intelligence, sensitivity and education to the dangerous field of overseeing caged criminals. Studies bear this out. They show that only one out of two guards in the nation's prisons is even a high school graduate, and only one out of three has been to college; not graduated, either, just attended. A Rhode Island college professor named Allan Berman did a survey of a hundred applicants for jobs in that state's prisons and found that most of them showed "emotional shallowness, alienation from social customs, and relative inability to profit from social sanctions."[10] The University of Rhode Island's psychology department also tested correctional officer applicants against prison inmates to see the "violence potential" of each. The tests showed the two groups were almost identical, with the guards coming out more violent than the inmates. "The officer group actually has the potential for even more unexplained lashing out than does the inmate group...the officer candidates are as likely as the inmates to engage in assaultive behavior."[11] In congressional hearings, too, evidence has piled up to prove that the occupation of correctional officer "appeals to those who like to wield power over the powerless and to persons of sadistic bent."[12] For the ridiculous wages paid—even in 1980 the starting salary for a guard at the Penitentiary of New Mexico was a lowly $765 a month—it's understandable that the only reason a man would take the job would be out of desperation or hate.

Hate is just a short jump away from the judgmental, holier-than-thou attitude that formed the concept of the American penitentiary. In 1787, Philadelphian Dr. Benjamin Rush walked into good old Ben Franklin's home and proposed that the "right way to treat offenders was to make them repent their crimes...offenders should be locked alone in cells day and night, so that in such awful solitude they would have nothing to do but to ponder their acts, repent, and reform."[13] From Dr. Rush's idea evolved "the Auburn system," the model for the penitentiary of today. That system added a sadistic twist to Dr. Rush's original notion. Elam Lynds, the first warden of Sing Sing, which was built in 1825, summed up the philosophy that has guided the thinking of corrections officials in this country for the past 150 years: "Reformation of the criminal could not possibly be effected until the spirit of the criminal was broken."[14]

Quite the opposite has proven to be the case. If there's been any reformation at all from the prison experience it's been to turn petty thieves into killers and lifetime residents of the nation's penitentiaries. Reformation: ask any warden or guard or prison administrator what he thinks about the possibilities of reformation or what his true opinion of a convict is. If you catch him in a rare moment of honesty, he'll tell you that he sees the inmate as something less than human and punishment as the only thing that works to keep him in line. The law itself upholds this view. When a person is convicted of committing a felony, he forfeits all individual rights: he is in a state of civil death. "He has, as a consequence of his crime, not only forfeited his liberty, but all his personal rights except those which the law in its humanity accords to him. He is for the time being the slave of the state."[15] The courts have interpreted the Thirteenth Amendment as it applies to law breakers this way: "Neither slavery nor involuntary servitude, *except as a punishment for crime whereof the party shall have been duly convicted,* shall exist within the United States." Because the law of the land holds that a convict is in this state of civil death, the courts likewise uphold the autonomy of the prison administrators in running the country's penal institutions. They have ruled that "courts are without power to supervise prison administration or to interfere with the ordinary prison rules or regulations."[16] Once the gates of the animal farm close around a person convicted of committing a crime, he answers only to the law of the poorly paid, emotionally shallow, alienated, potentially violent, sadistic men who, studies have shown, flock to the field of corrections. Maybe the old way of treating criminals, before the penitentiary system was instituted, is more humane. Certainly it more honestly reflected the attitude of society toward those who broke its laws. If you committed a crime in the early days of America, you were going to feel the revenge of the citizenry. You'd be beheaded or hanged, flogged, stretched on the rack, tortured, blinded, tarred and feathered, ridden out of town on a rail or spread-eagled in the stocks for all to gape at. No one pretended they were trying to reform you; they were just giving you your due reward for acting in violation of the community's codes. And it was an instant reward. If your crime didn't warrant beheading or hanging, you had an opportunity to resume your life with the immediate scar of that punishment to remind you of the folly of your old ways. Today, the psychological scars of years of mental and physical torture wipe out any thought of conforming to the society that allowed them to be inflicted. A convict conforms more to what the prison experience teaches: to behave as brutally as those who wield the power and run the institution. I'm certainly not suggesting we go back to the rack or the stocks. I'm just saying that we still haven't found a way of dealing with the so-called criminal element in our culture.

People have been trying to find out what makes a person become a criminal for at least the past two hundred years; maybe forever. Many theories have been expounded, but all have been rubbed out by each generation's new ideas on the subject. It used to be thought that the devil was to blame. In the nineteenth century, the English accused criminals of "being prompted and instigated by the Devil."[17] In 1862, the North Carolina Supreme Court followed its ancestors' train of thought by declaring: "To know the right and still the wrong pursue proceeds from a perverse will brought about by the seductions of the Evil One."[18]

Toward the end of the nineteenth century, Italian criminologist Cesare Lombroso took the blame away from the devil and gave it to God. Criminals are born that way, he said, "not a variation from the norm, but practically a special species, a subspecies, having distinct physical and mental characteristics."[19]

In the 1930s came another theory, from a German this time. His studies showed that certain physical types were more drawn to crime than others: men who were stout and squat and had large abdomens were usually the occasional offenders, while slender men with slight, muscular builds were most often habitual criminals.

The 1940s expanded on this with the gland analysis that named the criminals of the world 'mesomorphs.' In physical type, the mesomorph was the reverse of the previous decade's description of a criminal. Instead of short and fat, the criminal was now thought to be muscular, bear-like, assertive, noisy, and aggressive.

During all these speculations on the physique of the criminal, the doctors who were engaged in the budding new fields of psychology and psychiatry were putting in their two cents worth. In 1920, a Princeton psychologist, Dr. Henry Goddard, thought that criminals were people of low mentality, but by 1959 that theory was soundly disproven. "Studies of prison populations made by clinical psychologists demonstrate that those behind bars compare favorably with the general population in intelligence. Since we seldom arrest and convict criminals except the poor, inept, and friendless, we can know very little of the intelligence of the bulk of the criminal world. It is quite possible that it is, by and large, superior."[20] Indeed, it is currently held that the criminal mind and the creative mind are but two sides of the same potential, the one being undeveloped, uneducated and frustrated. More than just the "poor, inept and friendless" have criminal minds. In the late 1940s, 1700 anonymous New Yorkers, all in the upper income bracket, who'd never been arrested, answered questions about their criminal activities. It turned out that 91 percent of them—64 percent of the men and 27 percent of the women—had committed a felony for which they could have been sent to the state pen had they been caught and convicted.[21]

Nevertheless, poverty, it was clear even to theorizers in 1870, was and remains the major factor in the making of a criminal. In the 1870s the prisons were filled with Irish and Italian immigrants, the young, the poor, and Native Americans. Today the prisons are filled with the new immigrants the country takes in with open arms, open arms that close the moment the boat lands; with our own slum dwellers, with blacks, Chicanos, and poor whites who are disenfranchised by society, as well as young counter-culture drug users. Why is it the poor are more likely to end up in jail, while the more affluent middle class who are committing as many felonies aren't? It's not just a matter of lack of money for legal fees, because the middle-class whites aren't even apprehended for their crimes. It's been demonstrated so much in our society of late that it's almost redundant to say it, but the police instantly react to blacks and other ethnic minorities as if they were already criminals. In a book called "The Myth of the Criminal Type," the author, Professor Theodore Sarbin, writes:

> The belief that some classes of persons were "dangerous" guided the search for suspects.....Laws are broken by many citizens for many reasons: those suspects who fit the concurrent social type of the criminal are most likely to become objects of police suspicion...To account for the disproportionate numbers of lower-class and black prisoners, I propose that the agents of law enforcement and justice engage in decision-making against a backcloth of belief that people can be readily classified into two types, criminal and non-criminal.[22]

The President's crime commission confirmed that this was common practice in a 1967 report:

> A policeman in attempting to solve crimes must employ, in the absence of evidence, circumstantial indicators to link specific crimes with specific people. Thus policemen may stop Negro and Mexican youths in white neighborhoods, may suspect juveniles who act in what the policemen consider an impudent or overly casual manner, and may be influenced by such factors as unusual hair styles or clothes uncommon to the wearer's group or area...those who act frightened, penitent, and respectful are more likely to be released, while those who assert their autonomy and act indifferent or resistant run a substantially greater risk of being frisked, interrogated, or even taken into custody.[23]

For all this, we still haven't determined the root cause of the making of a criminal. The thread that runs throughout every finding, though, is poverty: financial poverty, opportunity poverty, educational poverty, love poverty, and finally, self-worth poverty. All these begin in childhood. With the majority of criminals who get caught, there is a pattern of one kind of neglect or another in their early family life. My own beginnings are an example. I have certainly known convicts who suffered far more than I did in childhood, but the result is the same: a self-hatred that cannot be tolerated, that must be projected onto the world at large because the pain is too great to face. For most people, but especially for men in this society, anger and rebellion are the response to the wounds of early conditioning.

I never really knew my mother or father, particularly my father. He was an alcoholic and died of cirrhosis of the liver after I started my criminal endeavors. When I was three years old, my parents divorced and my mother put me in a foster home. I don't know whether she didn't want me or couldn't take care of me. I never gave it much thought, so it didn't bother me. In other words, I buried my feelings. The family I was farmed out to treated me well enough. They were a German couple who already had grandchildren my age. They were very strict but fortunately not mean. There were no beatings, but no affection either. My foster father didn't provide much of a male figure for me to learn from. He worked nights as a baker, came home as I was going to school, said hello, and that was the last I'd see of him until the next morning. My childhood was lifeless, with no emotions of either love or hate, within myself or from others. I deadened my feelings as I saw everyone around me deaden theirs. I spent fifteen years of empty time waiting to grow up and be on my own.

At fifteen, I joined the army with a fake ID. When I came out at eighteen with an honorable discharge and a few hundred dollars in my pocket, I felt like the world owed me a living. I had no desire to work. Finding a job wouldn't have been easy anyway. I didn't have a high school diploma—I'd left school after finishing the ninth grade. I had a complex about the way I expressed myself, knowing I sounded ignorant. I didn't really have a trade, at least not one I wanted to work at. I'd done some welding and plumbing in the army, but I'd had enough of it. I wanted to do something I hadn't done before. I wanted to be out in the world. Finally I decided hitchhiking around the country would satisfy my itch for freedom. It did, until one morning when I woke up in a Las Vegas motel room with seventy-five cents in my pocket, feeling broke and desperate with nowhere, and no one, to turn to for help. I reasoned that with only seventy-five cents to my name, the need for money seemed more immediate than the need for a job, which would take days to find: a simple robbery seemed the best solution. Fate presented me with the opportunity not five minutes later.

As I walked into the motel lobby to spend fifty of my seventy-five cents on a pack of smokes to help me scheme a plan, I saw the manager counting out the money from the night's receipts. I thought: this is as good a time as any. I took out the pocketknife I carried, walked up behind him, put the knife to his back and told him it was a stickup. He handed me the money without any fuss, and got down on the floor until I left, as I told him to. I walked out and got on the first bus out of town. I scored eight hundred dollars, more than I could legitimately earn in six weeks. It seemed so easy; I kept on pulling bigger and bigger robberies, rationalizing that I'd continue stealing only until I figured out what I really wanted to do in life. Life doesn't work that way though. Three and a half years after I started my criminal career, I got busted.

Those first nine years in the penitentiary didn't do anything to change my mind about crime. When I was finally paroled, after becoming one of the hardcore cons, it took only fourteen months for me to sink into the despair that led me to robbing so many years before. It was Christmas, I'd lost my job and my girlfriend, and I was down to my last thirty dollars. I felt like I had nothing to lose even if I did go back to Santa Fe. Which I did. It was as if life were taking me by the scruff of the neck and saying, "Look, you sorry sucker, you're going to learn some lessons whether you like it or not." And learn I did in the next five years, but not because I had any help from either prison officials or inmates. If it takes fourteen years for a penitentiary to reform a man's way of thinking, something's got to be wrong with the system.

One of the major things wrong with it is the absence of normal sexual relations. It's perverse to lock up men in their sexual prime and not provide a normal outlet for their erotic desires. We're dealing with passionate, needing, angry men here, not saints and ascetics ready to take up celibacy. Further, the softness of a female would do a lot to calm down the furies that rage inside an inmate. Not only do prison authorities forbid sexual relations between men and women, they have tight restrictions on how much a man can simply *kiss* his own wife or his girlfriend during visits. The appetites will be satisfied, though, even if reluctantly. It took me five years to succumb to the advances of a jailhouse queen. During those first five years, I relied on my right hand and my fertile fantasies, like so many inmates do. But there's no privacy in prison; masturbation, like sex, has to be public, or snuck in corners of darkness. I didn't like myself being with a man sexually, or being seen doing it with him, so I soon stopped having sex with the queen, and returned to my solitary pleasures. Many did like being with men, however; many, who would not be with them on the street, used them in prison to work out their anger along with their orgasms. Rape was the going mode of sexual fulfillment in the prison population, in every prison:

> Prison rape contributes heavily to the ethic of force that dominates every prison. The patterns of prison sex, in fact, raise sharply the question whether a former prison medical officer has called "forced segregation of dangerous individuals within a small perimeter" makes any sense at all. These sex patterns are one more assurance that most inmates will leave prison more antisocial than they were when they entered.[24]

I was initiated into the ritual of prison rape on my first night in population, fortunately as an observer. Some noises near my bunk woke me. When I opened my eyes, I saw three black inmates standing over the dude in the bed next to mine. We'd both just come out of Quarantine, and, like me, he was young and white. His eyes were wide with fear. One of the blacks held a large knife over his head. "Roll over, boy," he said. The kid had no choice. I'll never forget the look on his face as he turned over onto his stomach. He was naked except for the sheet that covered him. The black with the knife pulled the sheet down and mounted him, thrusting his huge cock into the poor guy's asshole with no pity and no grease to ease the pain. He had to cover the kid's mouth to stifle his screams. When the first one was finished, the other two took their turns. By then the guy's muffled screams had turned into humiliated whimpering. When all three were finished, they returned to their beds at the other end of the dormitory. I lay there without moving, just listening to the kid's quiet crying. I stayed awake the rest of the night. It was then I swore I'd become such a hardcore con that no one would ever come near me like that.

# 9

*A prison film after Fellini. Fade in...enter the Archbishop. The Archbishop of Santa Fe...is given a tour of the prison by abject officialdom. When he emerges, he is surrounded by his parishioners, overwhelmed, almost, by shouted questions. What has become of my husband? My son? You will be pleased to know, he tells them that...amid all the rubble, smashed cellblocks, burned gymnasium, the chapel had been spared. This is a powerful indication, he tells them, of the love of God, the faith in Jesus, that still fills the hearts of the prisoners. But what of my husband? My son? The archbishop silences their questions, spreads his hands. Let us pray. The archbishop turns away from the crowd. Behind are the questions he cannot answer. Inside is the carnage he dared not be first to reveal. Water. Fire. Powdered toilets. Charred relations. The stabbed, the hanged, the cleaved—dead in their own excrement...The parishioners remain by the highway, where they have stood for many hours—men, women, children...there is no place to sit but the rocky ground; there is no place to relieve oneself. Of anything. But such things are temporal; they are not of the spirit. People may be dead inside, their screams still hanging on the walls, but God is alive and well in the gleaming chapel. The archbishop drives back to town. The camera follows him. Sooner or later it will catch him washing his hands.*

—Robert Mayer [1]

## Saturday, February 2, 1980.

The massacre of the men in Cellblock 4 went on until mid-morning. All over the penitentiary the screams of the tortured victims could be heard, interspersed with radio transmissions announcing things like, "We just killed five more down here!" Only the strongest stomachs were able to stand the smell of burning flesh that permeated the air, especially in the units on the north side, where I was. I saw a lot of men bend over and puke their guts out. It wasn't only the burning flesh, it was the whole scene that was becoming repulsive, and the sickening, fatty stench punctuated it. It wasn't until 10:30 or 11:00, three and a half to four hours after the death squad had entered the protection unit, that the screaming stopped; though the smell of burning flesh never left the atmosphere.

I was about to go down to the hospital to find some aspirin when an old friend of mine walked into the old men's dormitory and asked if we had any coffee. I gave him some and he and I sat down and started rapping. He looked like he'd just come out of a Viet Nam raid, his face smeared with black soot and blood, his hair a matted mess, his prison fatigues covered with splotches of dried, brown blood. Then I spotted a screwdriver sticking out of his back pocket.

"Hey, that screwdriver in your pocket there," I said, "it looks like it's got some blood on it."

"Yeah, got me a few down in 4," he bragged.

"Well, what happened? Run it down."

And he did, describing in full detail the killings he'd seen his buddies participate in, plus his own deeds. He'd stabbed three men in the chest with his screwdriver, bashed in another's head, and burned a guy alive by throwing gasoline into his jammed cell.

While he was talking, I started thinking. I'd come a long way in fourteen years. Even six years ago I might have given some thought to paying back a snitch or welcher. Ten years ago I gave it more than a thought; I actually shafted a dude who'd run off with our dope money. Fortunately, though I didn't think so at the time, he didn't die. As I listened to this man go on about the murders he'd seen and committed in Cellblock 4, I knew that even then I wouldn't have participated in what he was describing. A sickness had taken those men over, and I thanked God I hadn't been infected by it, this time or any time. Still, I had to keep up my hardcore front with my old friend here. I'd known him a long time in the joint, but if he'd gone as overboard as he was saying who knew when he'd snap on me. I couldn't tell if he was slurring his words because of drugs or fatigue, but in either case he'd be hypersensitive, especially after using me as a confessional.

"Man, I would've been down there with you," I tried to explain, "but I got my parole comin' up in two months."

"I can dig it, bro, just keep your eyes open. Anyone thinks you been sittin' on your ass up here and hiding out's liable to kill you if they catch you by yourself. We've finished with what we set out to do in 4, but there's a lot of other guys out there in population getting' knocked off right now. Just make sure you covered your back if you do step out into it."

I finished my coffee, thanked him for the advice, and got away from him as fast as I could. I gathered several friends from the dorm, and together, with extreme caution, we embarked into the madness. First we hit the hospital, not for anything more exotic than the aspirin I'd been needing for two hours. Then we made our way down to the kitchen to try and get some food. My headache was not only from revulsion but from hunger; we hadn't eaten anything since six o'clock the night before. Getting through to the kitchen was no easy task. The corridor was filled with doped rioters shouting and hollering at each other, stampeding back and forth in the smoky haze. We found very little food. The kitchen had been totally trashed and raided. Some cans of tomatoes had been left and we were happy to have them, though they were one of our least favorite foods when the prison served them. On our way back we stopped to take a look at Cellblock 4. I had a friend there and wanted to find out what happened to him. I didn't locate him. I got lost in the bodies and blood strewn all over the place; corpses hanging from the railing, sticking out between the bars of a cell. I saw one man hanging on a door with a rod through his skull, another with his genitals lying next to him. These sights, and the odor of shit and burned flesh that filled my nostrils, made me want to run out and away, but I forced myself to go through the tier and see for myself the devastation.

There is no way I can transmit the full horror of that scene, and there's no way I can erase it from my mind. My only point in recounting in detail the savagery of this riot, in putting violent imagery in other minds, is to etch the picture of prison life as it really is into the public opinion, etch it so indelibly that people can never erase from their consciousness the consequences of inhumane treatment. Think of it: though my screwdriver-wielding executioner friend is a lifer, he's eligible for parole after he's served ten or fifteen years of his sentence. He'll be out on the streets again—after all he's learned about being the most violent dude on the block in the pen, after murdering four men in this riot—sitting next to you on a bus, maybe. What has your tax money taught him during his ten years in prison, in terms of dealing with life? It's taught him to hate, to steal, to fight, to kill. If you look at him wrong and he's feeling depressed, or if he's broke and you look flush, he's more than likely to use one or all of those talents on you.

Your tax dollar also teaches inmates to rape their own sex and take their most sublime ecstasy in an act of violent sodomy. James Foley was a nineteen-year-old peach-fuzzed kid from Albuquerque who came into the penitentiary in December 1979 to do a life sentence for the first-degree murder of the manager of a Circle K store he robbed. Foley was big—six-foot-four, two hundred pounds—and, like most kids when they first enter the joint, he tried to cover his youth and fear by acting tough. For James Foley, it didn't work. The first week he was in population he was beaten by a group from the Chicano clique. The administration locked him up in Protection for a few weeks, then made the mistake of putting him back in population a week or so before the riot. It didn't matter why he'd gone to Protection; the very fact that he'd wound up there made him a punk in a convict's eyes. In the midst of the riot on Saturday afternoon, that same group of Chicanos found him again, sitting on his bunk in Dormitory A-1, trying to stay out of everyone's way. As he saw the eight rioters approach his bed wielding pipes and bats, he became terrified and started crying and begging them not to bother him. They answered by telling him to take off his clothes. He did, mistakenly thinking obedience would save him. When he was naked, they told him to lie down on his side and clasp his hands under his knees. They tied his wrists together, binding him in this fetal position, then turned him over onto his stomach; and each of these eight barbiturated men took their turn sodomizing James Foley while the others whacked him severely with pipes and bats. When they'd all had their sexual satisfaction, they pushed him off the bed and continued the beating, kicking him in the head and kidneys until he was unconscious. Later it would be discovered that he was more than unconscious. They had kicked James Foley to death.

This once small band of rapists, their number now increased by other rioters who'd joined in the beating of James Foley, turned their attention to the other residents of the dormitory. They had watched Foley's rape in fear for their own safety. A-1 was a unit where the younger inmates in the prison were housed. They had thought that by staying out of the way they would be safe and had not armed themselves. Each of these young convicts was tied in the same fetal position as Foley, each had a pillowcase placed over his head, and each was sodomized more than ten times. Whenever they made a move or a sound, a pipe or fist would hit them over the head. They were dimly aware of the sounds of moaning going on around them, but not until their rapists had gone on to greener pastures, and the first of them untied and unhooded himself, was it clear to them that their dormitory had been turned into a battlefield brothel that would have shocked the father of sadism himself. After the riot was over, one of these rape victims talked to a reporter. He was telling his story, he said, because he wanted to let America know that inmates get raped by other inmates all the time in every prison in the country. He wanted to tell it "so the public will be enlightened."[2]

While the rapists stalked the prison for more perverse ecstasy, other rioters wandered through the hallways and dormitories looking for vengeance on old enemies. In prison it takes only small incidents to make a man form a vendetta against a fellow convict, and under the influence of drugs and freed anger, these grudges seemed worth killing for. Not all the payback dished out was fatal, and relatively few took part in these random revenge murders. In all, only twenty-five, including the dozen or so Cellblock 4 executioners, participated in the killings;

but they ended more than thirty lives. In the light of the sober days to come, these payback attacks seemed senseless even to many of the perpetrators. One inmate was killed because he'd gone out with his murderer's girlfriend ten years before. Another had his eye gouged out, yet another had one testical cut off. Both lived to remember the moment and carry the scars. An inmate carefully winding his way down the main corridor to the safety of Dormitory E-2—the only unit in the entire building that was left intact, where men who wanted to mind their own business could just sit around, drink coffee, and play cards—bumped into someone accidentally because the smoke was so thick he couldn't see. The next thing he knew was the heavy, cold feel of steel rods pounding on his head. Fortunately, he saw a meat cleaver coming at him in time to ward it off with his arm. The cleaver caught him on the wrist and cut clear through to the bone. The gashes on his head and arm bled profusely into the many towels a self-styled inmate paramedic kept wrapped around them until medical attention was available hours later. It got so frenetic that these wandering gangs became even less particular about who they attacked. If a man was walking alone, the gangs, in their convoluted thinking, would consider his very vulnerability a worthy reason to beat him and teach him a lesson about the folly of weakness. Lust for "sniff" was also a reason to kill. Two men had just gotten a jar of shoe glue from the shoe shop in the basement and were walking upstairs with it when a group of five Chicanos standing at the top of the stairs saw them and demanded they turn over the precious solvent to them. The two refused and the larger group beat it and their lives away from them. There was some instant karma, too. One of the rape squad got his throat cut a few hours after he'd satiated himself in Dormitory A-1. He lived, but spent a lot of hours bleeding and wondering if he would.

The majority of rioters who were not involved in these surges of rage upon their fellow convicts turned their energy to tearing apart the prison itself, setting fires everywhere, breaking everything they could get their hands on. Some found safe havens, like Dormitory E-2, while others merely took their chances, staggering around the hallways in a blind euphoria that hopefully made tolerable the beatings they inevitably suffered. The smarter inmates looked for a way out of the institution. They knew they were taking a chance going outside. No officials had said, "If you want to come out, do it, we won't shoot." They had no idea what was waiting for them out there, but they knew it couldn't be any worse than the chaos closing in on them inside. About twenty men who'd escaped from Cellblock 4 had the wits to grab one of the acetylene torches on their way out and head straight for the empty Cellblock 5 across the hall. They used the torch to cut a hole in a metal door on the east end of the unit and made a hasty retreat, surrendering at the front gate in the yard. When the rioters realized that inmates were getting out, they stationed a group to guard the opening and prevent anyone else from leaving. They got there in time to stop the Black Muslim leader and thirty of his men from going through. The Muslims weren't going to be stopped, however. They found out about the escape of the E-1 residents earlier and headed over to the south side dormitory. There, too, rioters stood guard, but this time the Muslim leader was determined. "Move aside," he demanded, "we're movin' out."

"The hell you are," the rioter answered, his bat poised to swing.

The Muslim leader was fast, and knocked the rioter to the ground with the billy club he was carrying. A few of his group took care of the rest of the guarding inmates and the opening was cleared. The blacks went through the hole one by one, with the leader out first, announcing to officials that he and his group were surrendering. Nothing was going unavenged this day, though. The rioters managed to stab the last two blacks to climb out, wounding them but not stopping their escape.

At 1:30 in the afternoon, twenty minutes after the Muslims surrendered, another twenty inmates found their way out. Throughout the rest of the day, men were breaking out of the penitentiary in groups and alone, through any opening they could find, often fighting the rioters who blocked their way. Many of those escaping were injured: cut and beaten either by the inside rampage or while trying to leave. Timing was with the wounded who had escaped. Two National Guard medical support teams, the 744 Medical Detachment and the 717th Medivac Helicopter Unit, had arrived at the front gate just before 1:00 P.M. The helicopters quickly transported the more seriously injured to St. Vincent Hospital in nearby Santa Fe, then transferred the more stabilized patients to Albuquerque medical facilities. As more inmates surrendered, the tents set up by the medical support teams filled with cases of bone fractures, amputations, and deep shock. Soon drug overdoses became the number-one malady these teams were treating. Inmates coming out of the prison would carry wounded and OD'd and unconscious rioters out into the yard up to the front gate, where the medics stationed behind the fence could get them once the gate was opened. Some of the convicts doing the carrying did so just as an excuse to get out, but a few stayed with the rioters, functioning as paramedics inside the prison, treating the wounded, hostages included, and repeatedly manning stretchers to get the seriously hurt to safety and medical care.

The gatehouse at Tower 1, in front of the penitentiary, had become not only the administration command post but a makeshift interrogation center where unwounded inmates, and later, released hostages who were physically able, were debriefed. The surrendering convicts were told to walk up to the front gate ten at a time, with their hands on top of their heads. The gate would be opened, they'd be let into the ten-foot moat of land between the two perimeter fences and told to line up with their hands on the fence. Corrections officers, and any other officials handy in the confusion, frisked them. Razor blades, homemade shanks, scissors and pockets full of pills were found. All weapons were tagged and placed in a large box, a box that reporters and officials wandering into the gatehouse would sift through curiously throughout the riot and for days afterward. When this frisking was over, the prisoners would be handcuffed with plastic wire and taken into the gatehouse for questioning. Anyone whose weapon showed telltale traces of blood was handed over to police for special interrogation elsewhere. After the debriefing, some of the men were sent to the warm walls of the Annex, where women inmates were usually housed. But the unit filled quickly, and soon there was nowhere else for them but the ten-foot-wide moat of fenced in but not sheltered land that surrounded the smoldering penitentiary. These early debriefings didn't net officials much information about the hostages, but they did give them the first verification that killing was taking place inside. Dr. Marc Orner was one of the group conducting the debriefing. Despised as he was, he got enough information from the twenty men who'd broken out of Cellblock 4 to be able to identify fifteen to twenty inmates as those doing the murdering, and to compile a list of ten "death squad" members.

There were hostages being released, but they were not in a condition to be questioned. The first was Officer Elton "Bigfoot" Curry. As the Cellblock 4 snitch slaughter was beginning at sunrise, Curry's beaten, stabbed, naked body was taken to the main entrance on a mattress. The rioters had doubts that he'd live, and they didn't want him dying in their hands. They knew their ex-warden, Felix Rodriguez, would be true to his word and storm the building if one of his guards died. Thanks to radio conversations with Captain Roybal and other officers being kept in the north wing, prison officials outside were assured that at least some of the remaining ten hostages were alive. The rioters had allowed Deputy Warden Montoya to speak with these guards to put power behind their demand that the penitentiary not be rushed. "At this moment, our lives are in your hands," Officer Larry Mendoza told Montoya, "what else can I say?" Montoya spent considerable time throughout the morning promising them that their safety was his main concern, that officials would take no actions that would jeopardize it.

At 8:20 A.M., Officer Mike Hernandez was carried out and handed over to medics, after an hour of haggling between the two sides of negotiators. All morning there were radio reports and snatches of conversations from inside the prison to the effect that Lieutenant Jose Anaya was in need of medical attention. An inmate called Doc, who was working as a paramedic, was overheard talking to another inmate on the radio: "I'm over here checking this Lieutenant Anaya," he said. "I think Anaya's got a concussion, and I think he's got a busted rib, and I know that he's got a heart condition and he needs to be moved, he needs to be taken out of here."[4] The rioters grabbed this opportunity to make a trade, and offered Anaya in return for Deputy Warden Montoya himself, or at least a medical doctor. The deputy warden refused the deal but offered them the carrot they most wanted: a meeting with the news media in return for Anaya. No agreement was struck, however. Lieutenant Anaya was left to the ministering of the inmate paramedic.

Because so many people were using the radios and confusing the transmissions, riot negotiators requested and got a field telephone for one-to-one communication with outside officials. The first person they called was the governor. They told him that the riot was started "just to get somebody's attention," and complained that they were being treated "like a bunch of kids,"[5] and asked for the opportunity to discuss their grievances with him, Deputy Warden Montoya, Deputy Corrections Secretary Felix Rodriguez, and the media. Governor King promised to set up a table for such a conference, in the prison yard, in one hour. The rioters in turn assured him no one was going to be hurt and they would give up the hostages by "three or four o'clock" that afternoon.[6] The governor reiterated that the prison would not be stormed. However, one riot negotiator didn't like the inclusion of Montoya in the conference, and called him to tell him so. "I talked to Bruce (King) a while ago and he said he was going to come down here and I would appreciate it if you didn't come down here with him."[7] Hearing this, other rioters with radios chimed in with their feelings about Montoya. "You've got fucking uncles, you've got brothers, and you've got cousins all working here and that is bad."[8] Through it all, Montoya stayed calm, responding only in the soothing manner he'd learned so recently at "hostage school."

Finally negotiations began in earnest. Inmate runners brought out their first list of demands and gave it to Felix Rodriguez at the front gate. The cement walkway from the prison building to the tower gate became the bargaining lane. Riot negotiators were guaranteed safety to talk face to face with officials, but through the crosswires of the perimeter fence that separated them. The first list contained six demands:

1. Reduce overcrowding

2. Comply with all court orders

3. No charges to be filed against inmates

4. Due process in classification procedures

5. Ten gas masks

6. Two new walkie-talkies [9]

They were given the ten gas masks and promises to consider the rest. Riot negotiators also requested that a doctor be sent inside the building to care for the mounting number of injured. Even Captain Roybal joined in this request, but Montoya insisted the wounded be brought outside for treatment. He did allow fire-fighters to go into the yard to put out the fire spreading through the administrative area, but when they approached the windows, they were driven away by rioters stabbing at the hoses with pipes and sharpened broom handles, even throwing gasoline.

While the institution burned, riot negotiators were writing up a fuller list of demands. They handed them to Rodriguez that afternoon. This time, officials gathered at the warden's residence to discuss strategy and determine what became these responses to that list:

1. Bring federal officials to the penitentiary to assure inmates no retaliation will occur.

ANSWER: We will ask for the assistance of the FBI.

2. Reclassify the men held in Cellblock 3.

ANSWER: Security risks will remain in Cellblock 3.

3. Leave all inmates in the units they were originally assigned to until uprising is over.

ANSWER: We cannot agree to this until the prison's condition is determined.

4. End overcrowding at the prison.

ANSWER: About 288 beds will be ready in July and we have asked for an additional 200 from the Legislature.

5. Improve visiting conditions at the prison.

ANSWER: This has been in effect for two weeks as worked out with the American Civil Liberties Union Negotiating Committee.

6. Improve prison food.

ANSWER: We will hire a nutritionist to oversee the food operation.

7. Allow the news media into the prison.

ANSWER: Not until all the hostages are released.

8. Improve recreational facilities.

ANSWER: We are now negotiating with the American Civil Liberties Union.

9. Improve the prison's educational facilities.

ANSWER: This is being discussed with the Legislature along with raising inmates' wages from the present twenty-five cents per hour.

10. Appoint a different disciplinary committee.

ANSWER: We will take a long, hard look at that.

11. End overall harassment.

ANSWER: We will have additional correctional officers who will be trained. The Corrections Commission is also looking at this problem.[10]

After receiving this, riot negotiators did not give up the hostages at "three or four o'clock" as they'd promised. The Corrections panel had both missed the point and skirted the issue in most of their responses. In asking for the media to have access to the prison, inmates weren't referring only to the immediate situation, but to the long run as well. They wanted the media to have general access to the penitentiary *in the future*, so that the public was constantly informed about conditions there. As it was, all media representatives were *personae non-gratis* at Santa Fe. And as for improvement in visiting conditions and recreational facilities being negotiated with the American Civil Liberties Union, inmates knew very well, from recent experience, that such negotiations were time-consuming and even when worked out, implementation was thoroughly resisted by prison authorities. Though the rioters who were doing most of the negotiation knew it was imperative to end the insanity going on around them, they also felt they could not give up with so little to show for the hell they'd been through, and the riot raged on.

At the State Capital in Santa Fe, where the Legislature was in the midst of its thirty-day session, Governor Bruce King asked ten key legislators to interrupt their legislative committee meetings and join him in his office. He needed their guidance on a decision he'd just made. In the interrogation of escaping inmates, accounts of the killing of a hostage guard had surfaced. In response to that news, the Governor had given orders to the National Guard and the state police to go in and take over the prison by force. He was waiting verification of the hostage's death to give the final word for the takeover to begin. All the legislators present agreed that he had taken the proper action. If there was killing of hostages, they told him, then it had to be stopped at all costs. The Governor thanked and dismissed them, in his rancher drawl, telling them he'd keep them informed, he should know something in thirty minutes or so. As the legislators walked out, three of the more progressive of them stayed behind: State Senators Manny Aragon and Tom Rutherford and Lieutenant Governor Roberto Mondragon. Manny Aragon broke the ice. He wanted to know if the Governor was going over to the prison to see for himself exactly what was going on. Aragon said he was sure there were a lot of innocent people who would be hurt if the prison were stormed. It took only a little more discussion for the Governor to decide to utilize their interest. He appointed the three to be his eyes and ears, to go to the penitentiary and find out if it was necessary to storm the building.

At 3:30 P.M. on Saturday, the three legislators met with police and prison officials, at the warden's house, to discuss the intelligence collected from inmates who'd surrendered. By that time, the rumor of a hostage's death had been discounted as false, and the Governor had been so notified. After an hour of discussion, Senators Aragon and Rutherford and Lieutenant Governor Mondragon drove around the perimeter fence of the penitentiary, to get a close look at the damage done so far. They saw more devastation than they'd expected. From the highway, smoke could be seen coming out of the building for miles, but up close they saw flames licking up the walls. It looked like a battlefield: wounded inmates being carried hurriedly to the front gate, medics running back and forth with stretchers to bring them to the medical tents stationed beyond the fence, helicopters flying in and out; and framing it all, the forlorn silhouettes of surrendered inmates standing, blankets wrapped around them, like dark ghosts between the perimeter fences.

It was five in the evening, the sun had set, and the chill of night air was approaching when the three legislators were dropped off at the gatehouse command post. Deputy Warden Montoya and Felix Rodriguez were negotiating face to face with inmates, and the three could hear pieces of the conversation from where they stood inside the building. But soon that little room got so crowded with interrogators, inmates and other officials that Senator Aragon decided to brave the night air and walked outside. Standing against the side of the building, Aragon was just a few feet away from the gateway to the area where Rodriguez and Montoya stood talking to negotiators on the other side of the fence. At one point, Felix Rodriguez turned toward the Senator and said, "Get me some batteries." Thinking of himself as merely a bystander, Aragon wondered whom he was talking to and didn't respond. When Rodriguez again asked for batteries, Aragon realized he was the only person around. He hopped to the request, went into the command post and brought out a box of flashlight batteries. The guard in the tower opened the gate so Aragon could hand the batteries to Rodriguez. Rodriguez took one look at them and said, "No, I need *radio* batteries." Back through the gate Aragon went, coming out this time with the right thing. When he turned to leave the negotiating area, he saw that the gate had been closed. Since he couldn't get out, he stood back against the fence and watched the negotiations proceed. Rodriguez didn't let him remain idle for long, however. "Get me a stretcher," he demanded. Aragon motioned to the guard in the tower to open the gate and again went to the command post, bringing out two stretchers this time. He put them down by Rodriguez's side, but when he turned to leave the area, the gate once more locked behind him. Asking for it to be opened just so he could get out didn't cross his mind. The situation was so tense that risking security simply for his own safety was out of the equation, particularly since he was able to be of use to the negotiators. Though he felt fear, he was fascinated with the events unfolding in front of him, and not unhappy that he had landed smack dab in the middle of them. As he stood watching the negotiations, it dawned on him that he knew the two inmate negotiators, and one of them rather well. He'd played Little League baseball with Lonnie Duran, the jailhouse lawyer who'd been responsible for writing up and winning a class action suit against the penitentiary. They'd grown up in the same neighborhood, the South Valley of Albuquerque. They exchanged greetings, and soon Senator Manny Aragon was taking part in the negotiations, with the blessings of Rodriguez.

The Senator was one of the best aids Rodriguez could have picked. Thirty to forty percent of the prison population came from Aragon's area, the South Valley, and many of his constituents were the fathers and mothers of these inmates. He'd helped many of them get in to see their sons and brothers and husbands in the prison and worked to get children special permission to see their fathers. The convicts knew him to be on their side. At every legislative session he introduced bills that would ease conditions and policies inside the penitentiary. In 1979, he'd sponsored a bill to study the possibility of conjugal visits, or at least furloughs. It didn't pass, nor was his compassionate attitude toward prisoners appreciated by his colleagues, the majority of whom voted the bill down. The preceding year, he'd introduced legislation calling for a raise in the pay of guards, but that, too, failed to pass, as did a bill to increase the number of parole and probation officers. These hadn't been good issues for him to go on in terms of his political career within the legislative circle, but still he remained true to his constituency. Now the chickens had come home to roost, and his so-called liberal interest in prisoner rights stood him in good stead. He didn't, though, pull any punches in talking to his old pals.

"Lonnie, what're you doing? You guys are crazy. You know you're not going to get away with it. Regardless of how this thing comes down, you know they're not going to negotiate with you on any leniency and stuff like that. I hope you're not involved in it..."

"I'm not..."

"Well, you've got to tell your friends in there that they're going to get nailed."

"How the hell do I tell them? They'll kill me. It's bad in there; they're killing a lot of people. There's no talkin' to them, they're all drugged up, that's the problem. They're just completely out of it. The only reason they let me out here is because they still remember they respect me, but, man, who knows when they'll black out and forget who I am?"

By 7:15 P.M., the negotiations had expanded. Rodriguez, Montoya, and Senator Aragon were joined by two news people, Santa Fe radio commentator Ernie Mills and Albuquerque television reporter John Andrews. The inmate negotiation team now included two Anglos: Donnie Stout and Michael Price. The talks became more heated with the addition of the two Anglos who trusted none of The Man's words. They negotiated the core of each side's demands: the official's demand for the release of hostages, the inmates' for a meeting with the news media. To appease the inmates, the two reporters had been brought in. Officials were still denying rioters the desired huddle with reporters in front of television cameras, but they hoped the presence of the newsmen would appease the negotiators enough to elicit the release of more hostages. Ernie Mills, a veteran political reporter covering the State Legislature, had been at the prison since dawn, the first newsman to arrive. He'd been observing the negotiations all day and had first talked with inmates late in the afternoon. Mills felt a special rapport with the prisoners. Due to his early background as a street kid in New Jersey, he felt he had some firsthand knowledge of the underdog's mind. He was aware that, with a convict, it was the little gestures that established trust. He took the time to estab-lish bonds of confidence by touching the men through the openings of the fence as they spoke, and by offering them cigarettes.

Progress was being made for both sides. With the go-ahead from Rodriguez, Ernie Mills promised that a television camera would be brought inside the insti-tution the next day. As a result of this promise, and their trust in the word of both Mills and Rodriguez, the rioters released Lieutenant Anaya, who had been reported in serious condition earlier in the day. At 8:22 P.M., Anaya was brought out of the building on a stretcher. Further negotiations promising a news confer-ence inside the penitentiary that night, brought the reluctant release of Officer Juan Bustos, who'd been made to crawl naked in front of the rioters at the start of the uprising. Even as the terms for his freedom were being defined, Mills and other negotiators could see the masked inmates who were guarding the front entrance stab and beat Bustos as others tried to get him through. He was finally brought out into the freezing night air at 11:20, naked and tied to a chair. Seven hostages remained inside the penitentiary.

When reporters showed up at the main gate, ready for the promised late night news conference, they were sent back to the highway entrance. Officials had decided that the mood of the inmates was too wild for the press to mix with. A little later, just as negotiations were about to shut down, an NBC cameraman from Los Angeles, Michael Shugrue, arrived at the gatehouse with camera in hand. He'd missed the first rush of reporters and would have been late had the conference actually taken place. He'd been delayed because he stopped at the NBC affiliate in Albuquerque to get a video recorder and camera for the session. Inmates at the gate saw Shugrue and asked if he would be willing to go inside alone and tape a conference with them. Shugrue was willing, providing officials were. "If you want to go in, go ahead,"[11] the deputy warden told him, but not before making a deal for one of the hostages in return for Shugrue's coverage. At seven minutes after midnight, Officer Michael Schmitt was carried out on a stretcher. But as the inmates approached the gate, they had a change of mind and turned around, dragged the hostage back toward the building, yelling to Mon-toya that they weren't releasing him until the reporter walked into the prison yard. When Montoya complied and Shugrue was in, Schmitt was again dragged to the gate. At first sight of his body, officials thought he was dead. He was lying on his stomach, naked, covered with dried blood. When Schmitt arrived at the hospital, he was alive but in critical condition.

The NBC cameraman spent about forty minutes inside the prison, video-taping rioters in the visitors' room of the administrative area. Some wore scarves covering their faces, others didn't. They spoke of all their complaints, from poor food to harassment by guards to lack of recreation. While they talked, Shugrue could hear radio transmissions among other inmates, warning of violent groups roaming the prison. "Be careful, take somebody that's armed and ready to fight…there are two groups in there that are going wild."[12] Killings were going on even as he was taping. True to their word, though, the rioters didn't harm Shugrue. When he was finished, he was escorted outside and through the yard without incident. "I was never threatened. I never saw a gun or knife, although there were a lot of clubs," he said afterwards. "If I had known then what was going on back there, I never would have gone in."[13]

When Sugrue left, inmate negotiators closed down talks for the night. "Attention all units," they radioed. "We're going to hold off till tomorrow morning. Make sure those guys are fed and nothing happens to them," Chopper One said, referring to the men who'd surrendered. "No hostages will be hurt. We'll start up again at eight in the morning."[14] The officials who'd been negotiating at the gate-house wearily closed up shop, grateful that they could get out of the bitter cold at last and go home to the warmth of a bed. In the moat where the surrendered inmates huddled trying to keep warm under thin blankets, there was no relief. The stench of the corpses that had been brought out of the prison into the yard, together with the smoke from the burning building, kept them remembering what they'd left. As did the screams of that night's victims.

## Sunday, February 3, 1980, 6:30 A.M.

By the looks of everyone and everything, this riot couldn't go on much longer. Yet, the killings continued. Still, the main riot negotiators remained the trusted spokesmen, unharmed and unhindered by their crazier rioting brothers; those who were tired of the holocaust continued to find their way out through every opening in the building. One group even had the heart to smuggle a young guard hostage out with them, twenty-two-year old Victor Gallegos, who'd only been on the staff for three weeks. What an initiation into prison life he'd had. After being blindfolded and stripped, he'd been placed in a cell with Captain Roybal. The captain was put on the bed, and Gallegos under it. The cell was locked and they both remained there for several hours, until other rioters smashed the door open and dragged the more visible Captain Royal out. "'I was praying the whole time,' Gallegos later told reporters, 'hoping they wouldn't find me.'"[15] They didn't, but he spent the next hours not knowing if they would or not. When the group who got Gallegos out of the prison first found him, they dressed him in an inmate's uniform and gave him an iron pipe, so he'd look like the other rioters, before they led him from the burning cellblock, through smoke so thick "you could only see two or three feet in front of you,"[16] to the outside. There were so many inmates finding their way out of the institution that one convict was overheard on the radio asking, "What the hell is going on? Where's everybody sneaking out of this place from?" By 8:00 A.M., a National Guard commander took a head count and reported that approximately eight hundred convicts were outside the building. Many of those walking, or being dragged, into the yard were suffering from serious drug overdoses. A few were violently resistant to the medical teams helping them, and had to be physically restrained. Helicopters chopped through the air overhead, picking up the wounded and the overdosed, flying them quickly to hospitals, clogging up emergency rooms with the tattooed bodies of convicts.

I escaped at about seven in the morning by carrying out a wounded inmate. I found his unconscious body on the stairs when I was on my way to take another quick look around. I brought him back into the dormitory and tried to bring him to consciousness, but he was overcome by smoke and seemed to be in a bad way. I figured that if I were ever going to get out, this would be the time. Covering my action by announcing that I was going to take the dude down to the information booth and dump him out the front door so he could get treatment, I put the body on my shoulders and carried it down through the smoke. As I passed the control center, some berserk rioter thought he recognized the guy I was carrying, and began swinging a baseball bat at his hanging legs. I didn't stop. When I finally got to the information booth, I recognized a few of the white and Chicano clique leaders gathered there.

"Hey, what's goin' on?" one asked.

I played my tough-guy role to the limit. "I got this punk on my shoulder, I think he's hurt. Open the door and I'll bounce him out so he don't get to stinkin' in here."

"Yeah, that's a good idea, get the motherfucker out of here. Is he dead?"

"Yeah, I think so," I answered, and without further ado headed for the door. When I was about three feet out, I yelled back, "I think I'll take him out a little further and dump him there." I walked about fifteen feet into the yard, laid him down on the cement walk, and kept on going.

I could hear a couple of Chicanos calling from inside, "Hey, *ese* (brother), where're you goin'?"

I just kept truckin', didn't look back or answer, until I heard one of my friends yell out, "Hey, Wally, what the fuck are you doin'?"

"I'm goin' out and I ain't comin' back," I yelled over my shoulder, "and if you had any sense you'd be out here with me."

As I approached the fence Rodriguez and Montoya stood on the other side of, I saw others who'd just surrendered lying on the grass, face down. I was about to do the same when Rodriguez yelled to me:

"Hey, Wally, you and the one next to you, go back and get that guy you brought out and bring him over here."

I cursed to myself but got up and did it, wondering all the way if someone would come out and shaft me. They didn't, and we safely carried the unconscious inmate up to the gate, where he was handed through to National Guard medics.

The guy helping me lay back down, but Rodriguez told me to come on out into the gatehouse area. My old caseworker was there, and he handcuffed me with a piece of plastic wire, then shook me down. Marc Orner and Felix Rodriguez interrogated me. They asked if I knew where the hostages were, if I'd seen them, what it looked like inside, were there any guns. They told me they'd heard there were eighty bodies in the gymnasium, but that was news to me. It turned out that these eighty weren't dead, just unconscious from drug overdoses. I told them that as far as I knew, no hostages had been killed. They'd gotten word that Roybal was dead, but I'd just seen him a few minutes before I came out. I assured them that there had been no word inside about the death of a hostage, that the people holding the guards knew the value of keeping them alive and the consequences of killing them. When they were finished questioning me, they took off the painful plastic cuffs and sent me inside the perimeter fence where the other surrendered inmates were. A few minutes later, their worries about Captain Roybal ended. At 8:15 A.M., anticipating the news conference promised the night before, two rioters brought him out to the front gate.

While the helicopter transporting the badly beaten Roybal to St. Vincent's Hospital whirred overhead, negotiations for the day began. Lonnie and Kedrick Duran and Vincent Candelaria spoke for the inmates, and Ernie Mills, Deputy Warden Robert Montoya, Felix Rodriguez, the brand-new Corrections Secretary Adolph Saenz and State Senator Manny Aragon bargained on the other side of the fence. This session managed to rile the ever-cool Deputy Warden Montoya.

He was getting a lot of abuse from inmates, and his tolerance level after thirty hours of tense control was at a minimum. The last straw began to be piled on when Lonnie Duran told his friend, Senator Aragon, that the cause of the riot was Montoya and his practices. This sentiment was borne out by many of the inmates in the yard. Rioters came up to the gate to say to one or the other of the officials negotiating, "Okay, you can have your hostages, just give us Montoya." The encounter that made the deputy warden break from his "hostage school" suave came from a rioter who, with tears in his eyes, said straight to his face and in front of his superiors, "Montoya, you chickenshit, you're the one who caused all this." No longer did he suppress his true colors. "You wait till this is over," Montoya answered, "I'll show you what shit can really go down." Senator Aragon overheard this and turned to Felix Rodriguez. "Hey, Felix, Bobby's losing it; you ought to get him out of here." Rodriguez agreed, and Montoya left the front gate area.[17]

A few minutes later, two more hostages came out. One had been released by riot negotiators, but the other had escaped from the rear of the prison with the help of a group of fleeing inmates. This left only two hostages in the hands of rioters.

At noon, a fight developed in the back of the yard, where rioters who hadn't surrendered but had left the building had been accumulating. A large group of Chicanos, wielding pipes and wooden planks, started chasing blacks, shouting, "Kill the niggers." The blacks ran to the sally-port gate, with the Chicanos close behind. Police outside the fence told the blacks to drop to the ground. When they did, the Chicanos found themselves staring into the aimed guns of twenty National Guardsmen and a warning that they had five minutes to retreat or be fired on. To the amazement of the Guardsmen, Superintendent of Correctional Security Manuel Koroneos intervened on the Chicanos' behalf, physically stepping in the line of fire between the guns and the inmates. The deputy sheriff in charge had to tell him to move or suffer the consequences. Koroneos moved, but only after being given a direct order. The Chicanos, bolstered by their homeboy security chief's action, still hadn't given up their position. It took another warning from the deputy sheriff and another look down the twenty gun barrels for them to disperse. The blacks were taken out of the yard and kept in an isolated section of the perimeter moat. This didn't stop the Chicanos or the whites from coming by and slinging verbal abuse, and often dirt and rocks, at them. In a bizarre synchronicity, just after this melee quieted down, the beheaded body of the only black killed in the riot, Paulina Paul, was brought out on a stretcher and placed against the side of the building, his severed head staring grotesquely between his legs. "If you don't get the media in here soon," one of the rioters who'd carried him out warned officials," the next one we shove out will be one of your guards and he'll be just like him."

Within an hour the riot negotiators had the televised news conference they'd been demanding for the past thirty-four hours. Ernie Mills and a cameraman from the local public television station set up an office in the gatehouse. Participating were inmate negotiators Lonnie Duran, Vincent Candelaria, and Kedrick Duran, along with four local reporters in addition to Mills, and intermittently, Felix Rodriguez. This was not a normal television interview. It was more an informal *TV verité*, with the three inmates voicing their concerns in tired, often slurring, voices. Obviously the lack of sleep had gotten to them; perhaps drugs too, at least in one case. All three sported mustaches, wool hats pulled over their ears, and prison-issued jackets. Throughout the session there were doors opening, people talking, and the punctuating sound of hiccups. Ernie Mills functioned as moderator, but there wasn't much moderating. The camera was turned on and the inmates took their turns talking through it to the public, who would see the uncut version on that night's news.

Lonnie Duran, the main inmate negotiator, launched the program. "The whole trip was, it wasn't an escape trip, it was just a trip to show the institution that we were not an evil mob. They were treating us like little children when we're grown up men."

Another inmate negotiator chimed in. "In other words, we're just tired of all this harassment, harassment, harassment; and it's not that they harass everybody, it's just a select few that they're just getting down on. Like, this is my second time here. When I was here the first time, I was harassed and harassed until I finally made a parole and got out of here. Now that I came back, I tried to do the best I could, but no, they wouldn't let me, they had to knock me off and knock me off for bullshit that I had nothing to do with. I wouldn't even go eat just to keep away from them."

"Another thing that has been brought up," Lonnie Duran took up his friend's thread of thought, "is they're trying to keep people in permanent segregation, as a program, but there's no college program in there, no good-time program, there's no program in there but bunk. I can see it if you commit a crime inside the institution, well, that's okay for it, but when you can get picked up for nothing without a report, well, then it's kind of hard for you to understand, it keeps you in limbo here, you know, like, two or three weeks you don't know what's happening then all of a sudden they come and say, well, you're turned loose. But, I don't think that's fair at all. If they got something on you, let's go do it and get it over with, but all this stuff about investigation just doesn't hit the spot."

"What's wrong with this penitentiary, I'll be truthful with you, is there is too many Indians and not enough chiefs."

"There's too many chiefs and not enough Indians," the third inmate negotiator interjected, slurringly.

"Well, all right, too many chiefs and not enough Indians, but I mean each captain has their own set of rules. At one time it was run by one captain and it ran smooth; under Mr. Rodriguez, when he was foreman, this penitentiary ran smooth. It was a great loss to us when we lost Mr. Felix Rodriguez. By all means, I know he won't take a demote in pay, but we need somebody with Mr. Rodriguez's caliber to run this penitentiary."

"I think pretty much that the three people involved in here have the same feelings as most institutions. All of us have been through it. Everybody's been griping about the same things, maybe if we got it cleared up it would be a lot better for all the institutions."

A reporter asked: "How much of the penitentiary would you say is on fire?"

"It's a total disaster, let's put it that way," Lonnie answered. "It's a total disaster because of the water leakage. The main water valve has burned, and there's water in every tier, except on the higher tiers, but there's water everywhere. You've got to walk through water."

The slurring negotiator droned in: "On the way out here right now, there's a man in between the two grills of the control center. I believe he's dead."

Again Lonnie finished his friend's train of thought. "You can tell by blood all over his face. But I know a personal friend of mine who died of smoke inhalation trying to get back to get another guy out, Frank Sedillo. He tried to go back to get somebody out and he's dead now. They still haven't, as of right now, taken him out. And I'm going to ask Mr. Felix Rodriguez, I'm pretty sure he'll give me permission, to get nine stretchers. We'll have to make a double take on that because there's about eighteen who are dead, and the hostages are doing fairly well. I go every ten minutes, fifteen minutes, to check on them. I don't run nothing in this penitentiary, I'm just doing my time, but yet, because I've got a college education, the guys want me to become the mediator…"

"The reason for the three of us to come in here is because we've been here a while and we've seen the changes that come down. It's not that we're something out of the ordinary, it's just that not too many people like to come and talk to The Man or anything, see? But if somebody don't come and do it, then it's got to be…"

"They're gonna just resort to more killing and I think there's been enough of this," the slurring negotiator interrupted. "Personally, myself, I don't want to see no more killings. I'd like to just get all this taken care of the soonest possible, the easiest way possible, without no more rioting."

The main negotiator changed the topic. "I go to mediation meetings once a month, and Mr. Rodriguez proposed this in our mediation hearings, but the Department of Corrections at the time didn't go along with it. Under Mr. Rodriguez's rule they had school release, work release, rehabilitative courses. This is what the penitentiary lacks: rehabilitative courses. Right now they've got a six-month waiting list to see a psychiatrist, and there's guys in there that are walking around like zombies. They've got them up on Thorazine, or whatever it is, walking like zombies that actually don't belong in the penitentiary, they belong in a mental institution. What I'm saying is, it kind of hurts me, because this renovation that's gone on, it's gone to the birds now because of what's happened. There's knee-high water all over the place…"

Ernie Mills broke in to tell them that what they were filming would be available not just to Channel 5, the public television station, but to all the networks "as long as that's what you guys want."

"As long as it's known that we aren't the ringleaders…"

""In fact, the three of us were in Cellblock 3 and we were brought out. Wherever it started, I don't know who or where…"

"You say you were brought out by other inmates?" a reporter asked.

"By other inmates. The three of us were all in Segregation, Cellblock 3. I still have my segregation coveralls on. I was on the north side, bottom tier, and he was on the south side."

"I was in the basement, what used to be Death Row, that's where I was."

Lonnie explained: "See, a lot of things you can't get around...You've got to watch out for your own interests. Even though you try not to get in deep, or at all, you're trying to do what's impossible, it's like sometimes you don't want to hook somebody, see, and you turn the other cheek and he still hooks you, see. So what are you gonna do?"

"Most of the guys feel the way you do about Felix?" Mills asked Lonnie.

"Yes. I believe I have Mr. Rodriguez's word and Mr. Montoya's word for no retribution or whatsoever, and I'm gonna take it at that."

"We were in Cellblock 3 and we were fast asleep when we heard this noise. They opened our doors, they told us: 'You come out and join in or you know what's going to happen.' We're just following our interests, you know?"

"Like, there's no way that we could have kept ourselves in the cell because they had cutting torches, and you'll see once you get inside, a lot of the cell bars are cut."

Ernie Mills directed the dialogue to the point of the negotiations: "What do you think the chances are that some of the hostages will come out when you go back in there after this?"

"They say they don't want to release the hostages, not unless they get to talk to the news media and Governor King."

"Is there any way possible that we can get a lawyer in here, make this all legalized?" the slurring one had the presence of mind to ask Rodriguez, who'd just come through the door. "That way, if something comes down—I'm not saying that maybe you'll go back on your word, 'cause I doubt it, or Mr. Montoya; but it's always better in black and white where we can say, well, lookit here, this is what they gave us, it's not just hearsay. You know what I mean? If you could arrange something like that."

"Well, if we do this," Felix Rodriguez responded, "whatever we negotiate at that time, then you guys would release hostages?"

Lonnie Duran answered for the group. "True, I'll do my damndest to have them released."

The other two didn't quite agree, however. "Once we release all the hostages, then we don't have no play besides your word," one complained.

Felix stoically agreed that was the case.

"Plus the fact that *we're* here," a reporter offered.

"And Felix hasn't gone back on his word with me yet," added Mills.

"Well, were you here the last time, when the men were marched, then stripped, with their hands over their head and everybody just hit them with billy clubs? Well, that's what happened the last time, that's the kind of retaliation that these inmates don't want. If they want to lock us up, lock us up and then later on we'll straighten out our differences."

On hearing that the tape was about to run out, one of the inmate negotiators brought up the injured inside the building. "There's men inside who need medical attention right now. There's about fifteen dead and about six injured that need sutures on their face; they're bashed in pretty bad. I know one who's soaked through two towels already. I told him, 'You need stitches on that, man.' He said, 'I can't go, they'll shoot me.' Right now while we're sittin' here there's probably killing going on..."

"I would like to see if I can get approval to get some guys to get some dead people out of there," Lonnie Duran said. "To get the inmates to get the people out of there, and the hurt people."

Rodriguez gave him the go-ahead, saying he could have all the stretchers he needed. A reporter asked the group at large: "Have you felt that your life has been threatened throughout the last twenty-five to thirty hours?"

"Well, I've really been trying to take care of the hostages," the slurring negotiator answered. "I was running back and forth to Cellblock 3 trying to get them towels, coffee, whatever they needed."

"The officers that are in our custody right now are most of the old-time guards that we know pretty good and they always treated us right; that's the reason they're getting treated right."[18]

The staccato whirring of a helicopter hovering overhead marked the end of the filming. The camera was reloaded and, along with the reporters and negotiators, moved to the sidewalk inside the prison yard in anticipation of the release of the hostages and the riot's end.

There were still more negotiation points the inmates needed settled, however. Joining Candelaria and the two Durans were inmates Michael Colby and Bill Stevens. Their main worry was retribution after the riot.

"One of our demands now is that the five of us that you've talked to are in jeopardy right now, no matter what they say," Colby told reporters. "Once you people leave and they go in there, they're going to beat us bad."

"It's on the camera and it's in the paper," Mills tried to reassure him.

Rodriguez addressed the cameras and reporters and made it real. "We will get the hostages out here. I have assured Colby and Stevens, the two Durans, and Candelaria that they will be transferred out of state tomorrow."

"And also that those who stay behind…"

"Won't be hurt," the ex-warden completed Colby's thought.

"No segregation?"

"Not at all."

"You can't put people in Cellblock 3 because there's no Cellblock 3 there."[19]

A few more minutes of haggling and everything was settled. The rioters could have what they'd asked for. Officials would do all in their power to transfer the negotiators to out-of-state prisons as soon as possible; nobody would be strip-searched or beaten after the penitentiary was taken; all in return for the remaining two hostages. The five inmate negotiators were to ask everyone to come out of the prison, move up to the gate, and bring the hostages along with them Then, one dormitory or cellblock at a time would be told to return to their unit and pick up their personal belongings. With these points agreed on, Duran and company went back into the prison to explain the deal to the approximately 125 inmates still inside. Soon they started coming out, with the two hostages in the front lines. But a helicopter swerved in and hovered low over the yard, triggering the convicts' innate distrust of The Man. Thinking they were being set up and were about to get shot down, they started running back into the building, dragging the hostages with them. "You lied to me, you lied to me," some of them shouted. The gate was open, and Senator Aragon ran into the yard, took off his jacket and used it to flag the helicopter away. Official radios, too, were busily trying to connect with the pilot. Finally the chopper lifted and whirred off, but by that time the inmates were back inside the dormitory, and so were the hostages.

Colby, Lonnie Duran and Stevens came out, angry. "What kind of shit is this, you fucker? What are you tryin' to pull?" they asked Aragon.

"Hey, we don't control those guys," the Senator explained. "Look at this place, it's a goddamned circus. We've got every branch of law enforcement in the state here; they're more disorganized on this side of the fence than you guys in there. Nobody's ready for this thing. The National Guard is marching around to keep warm, and every time they move, you guys get worried it means an attack.

Give us a break. You're hearing it from us, you're not going to get hurt, you're not going to get strip-searched, nobody's going to beat you."

It took forty-five minutes to get another agreement, but this time there was an additional proviso from the riot negotiators. "Before we tell you guys what's going on, we're going to go get our personal belongings first and come out; that way we can see what's going on. Then you'll get your hostages."

And so it was. The first of the five negotiators out of the building were Lonnie Duran and Vince Candelaria. The two remaining hostages were brought out and forced to sit in front of the prison, blindfolded, their hands tied behind their backs, surrounded by armed and masked rioters. Adolph Saenz, who'd been corrections secretary for just two days, suggested to Rodriguez that it would be a good idea to talk to Duran and Candelaria by themselves, away from the influence of the hardcore attitudes of Colby and Stevens. Rodriguez, who had been worried that Duran and Candelaria were losing their control of the negotiations, took the suggestion and called the two over to him. "Look, you know what's coming down. We've got an agreement, there's no problem, but before Colby and Stevens come out here and start raising hell again, why don't you guys get the last two hostages, turn them over to us, and then it's over." The two thought about it a minute, then walked over, took the hostages from the surprised inmates, and brought them to Rodriguez. The gate was opened, the hostages came through. Before the gate was closed again, Rodriguez addressed Duran and Candelaria: "You want to come out now, too? It would be better for you if you did." And they did. But the armed inmates who had been guarding the two hostages realized they'd been double-crossed and started yelling at Duran and Candelaria, "What the hell is going on here, you fuckers? You lied to us." Senator Aragon answered for his childhood friends: "Hey, man it's over. All the hostages are here, you can see it's over. You guys would be smart to put your stuff down, too. You're better off over here than in there." The inmates resisted for a few minutes, then saw the wisdom of the suggestion and came out. As to whether Duran and Candelaria betrayed the inmates, there was question. Warden Griffin and Deputy Warden Montoya said they thought they had, but Rodriguez didn't. "By that time everybody was fed up with the whole thing. The smoke was really getting to a lot of these people. They were just as tired of the damned thing as we were."[20]

When Colby and Stevens came out of the building five minutes later, they definitely felt betrayed. As they walked up to the front gate, Colby, with a baseball bat in his hand, was greeted by the hard words of Senator Aragon: "Hey Colby, it's over. The hostages are all out now." Colby dropped his knapsack of personal belongings, took three steps back, and started yelling for Lonnie and Vince, not believing what he'd heard. When the truth of it sunk in, he screamed furiously at the officials in front of him: "You lied to us! We're going back in!" Rodriguez took control. "Colby…you got a deal, we're going to live up to it, but if you start yelling for those guys to go back inside that penitentiary, these guards are going to blow your heads off. We don't want any more trouble. It's over. Just go sit down over there." It took a few more minutes of yelling back and forth, but finally Colby and Stevens reluctantly put their weapons down and accepted the inevitable. As state police and National Guardsmen rushed through the gates to overtake the prison the last radio transmission from the rioters was heard. It was in Spanish, between two inmates known only as Danny and Big Al: "The stupid asses give up the hostages. Now they're going to come in and shoot us. I'm up to my neck in this. If I'm going to die, I'm going to die like a man." Then a few minutes later, the same voice said: "They got us, Big Al. They got us good. They're lined up about thirty yards from us. If you can get word to the people inside, tell them to get out of there." Then Danny was heard talking to other inmates: "When we needed you guys, you turned your back on us. Now you're going to suffer. Tell them guys [presumably the Chicano negotiators] never to call me homeboy again or they're dead." [21]

What National Guardsmen saw when they went into the penitentiary caused one of them to remark to a reporter afterwards, "I was in 'Nam for two years, and like I've seen some hellacious sights over there, and it's my personal opinion and belief that these inmates out here made 'Nam look like a playpen."[22] The building was demolished. The mesh-reinforced concrete walls had been pounded in to make holes so the rioters could travel through the prison during the last hours of the riot. Fire and water damage had ruined the electronic locking mechanism of the north wing grills, which were jammed shut. Thick plate-glass shards were all over the main reception area; the air was filled with smoke and ashes; floating in the ankle-deep murky water were many corpses, gruesome sights, with heads so bashed in they were unrecognizable. But in Cellblock 4, the stench and sight were the worst. Senator Manny Aragon had followed behind the first contingent of Guardsmen, along with a small group of civilian observers. When he reached Cellblock 4, he didn't go in; one look was enough to turn him around. He didn't see the charred remains of bodies, the blood-splattered walls, the thick pool of bloody drag marks leading from the back of one cell to the railing outside; nor did he see the oddity of Cell 10, with its neatly made bunk bed, blanket tucked perfectly around the corners of the mattress, a picture-book reality that had no place in the blood and guts surrounding it. Instead, the senator made his way down the endlessly long, dark corridor, dark because fire and water had short-circuited the electricity. He walked through the smoky hallway, sloshing through the water, climbing speedily through the holes in the wall that were the sole access-way to the front entrance, stopping only when he was safely through the yard and out the gate.

After thirty-six hours, the bloodiest prison riot in the nation's history was over. Thirty-three inmates were dead, all at the hands of their fellow convicts, and more than a hundred were hospitalized. God knows how many more were mentally and emotionally traumatized by the experience. Nowhere in the annals of prison uprisings in this country has there been such an incidence of inmate-to-inmate violence. Even in Attica, where the 1971 riot left forty-three dead, only three inmates were killed by their fellow convicts.

It wasn't over for the relatives of the inmates, however. They'd been standing vigil in the freezing temperatures since dawn Saturday, waiting at the front entrance of the prison, near Highway 14, to hear how their loved ones were, if their brother or husband or father was dead or alive. They'd watched the black smoke billow out of the building, a quarter of a mile away, their fears mounting as each hour ticked by with no news. They'd taken to mobbing every ambulance and car that came and went through the entrance, hoping to get some shred of information. Two hours before the riot ended, the governor's press secretary posted an incomplete list of inmates known to be alive. Shouts of joy and wails of grief went up as the list was read. A woman who didn't find her brother's name on the list cried out, "Ohhh, my brother's dead."[23] She was comforted by the reassurance of others that it was too soon to tell, all the names had not been given. By Sunday afternoon, their grief had turned to anger. Homemade signs of protest were made and held aloft with their shouts: *"No more Atticas!" "Protect the prisoners!"* That night, a corrections official read off a list of names over a public address system. He announced that the list was of those alive, but many couldn't hear this, and when the name of their relative was called out, they started weeping and shouting. This list, too, was incomplete, going only to the letter *G*. One woman moaned, "How long, how long will it be, where is my brother?"[24] They would hold three more days and nights of vigil, huddling together for warmth and courage, accompanying each other to remote places where they could urinate or defecate in some privacy, for there were no toilet facilities nearby, only the wide expanse of desert and the two-lane highway that was part of the Land of Enchantment's Turquoise Trail. Not until Monday, when the pleas of priests reached the ears of prison authorities, was the Red Cross brought in with portable bathrooms and some food. On Monday and Tuesday nights officials came out and read another incomplete list of those alive, and again many broke down sobbing, either because they didn't understand that the official was reading the names of the living or because they didn't hear their relative's name and thought him dead. At least two families discovered the deaths of a son and a brother from a newscast before they were notified by prison authorities. A final accounting of those alive and those dead wasn't completed until March 6th. As a clergy member commented, "They just hadn't thought about the families."[25]

# 10

*At night I can still hear the screams, and the smell of burning flesh still lingers in the back of my mind... The next time our cries will be heard throughout the heavens above, and society will have to pay the price along with us.*

—Letter from inmates of the Penitentiary of New Mexico[1]

An anthropologist—mind you, an *anthropologist!*—and eleven of his students were called in to search for fragments of human bones in the six inches of ashes and rubble that covered the burned-out gymnasium's floor. The office of the medical investigator had put into operation its "disaster plan," designed to go into effect only when there were "three or more bodies that cannot be visually identified because the remains are skeletonized, badly decomposed, burned, or mutilated."[2] Never before in the five years since its inception had there been a need to put the plan into action. Besides the anthropologist and his eleven students, six dentists, the state's chief medical investigator, and many of his pupils, worked round the clock, taking as many as ten hours on each of the thirty-three autopsies they conducted. A refrigerated truck was parked outside the State Laboratory to temporarily store the corpses until the busy pathologists could dissect them. Autopsies usually take no more than two hours, but "because each body was that of a homicide victim with two or three assailants," Medical Investigator Dr. James Weston explained, "I knew that we would need to keep track of lots of evidence. First-degree murder charges will be filed in every one of the cases. All of our findings are going to be presented in court as these cases go to trial."[3] As to the motivation behind the brutal killings, Weston said, "The overriding picture that I got was absolute, unbelievable rage."[4]

In the yard, where the surviving inmates lived for three days after the riot, the rage had not subsided. On Monday, February 4, fifteen convicts had to be taken to St. Vincent Hospital as the result of overnight beatings, stabbings, and one gang rape so severe it left the victim in shock and emotionally scarred for months. The paybacks for non-participation in the uprising had begun; prison sex continued as usual. As well, there was fear of the execution squads. Some of those suspected of being part of it had been locked up inside the prison, in the relatively undamaged Cellhouse 6, but others still mingled in the yard. The remaining squad members knew many inmates had been questioned, but they had no way of knowing who had talked about what they'd witnessed. Though they were aware that convicts who'd been willing to give names and details were being kept either in the Annex or other jails for safekeeping, they knew too that many who'd furnished information were still in the yard population.

The conditions they were living under out there did nothing to alleviate the turbulence the prisoners felt. They had no shelter except the thin green army blankets supplied by the National Guard, and the first night there weren't enough of them to go around; another reason for fights and stabbings: "Give me your blanket or I'll pull your throat out." On Monday, when reporters came through to make a tour of the prison, the inmates complained to them that they lacked food and medical attention. "We got the blankets thirty minutes ago to make it look good for the press when they came in," one inmate shouted. "We've been out here three days with one hot dog." Another said all he'd had to eat or drink was one cup of water since Sunday.[5]

On Tuesday, Deputy Warden Robert Montoya let the leash off his own rage. Forgetting that he was surrounded by more than his protective clique, he let the state police who were guarding the prison witness his sadistic streak. Four inmates who were about to be re-housed in the penitentiary—as units were made accessible, the men were assigned to them—refused to go back, taking up wooden planks to aid their resistance. It wasn't just the memories the building held, they told police. They said they "feared for their lives if they went into the prison because they had spoken with state police interviewers."[6] Montoya joined with state police to get the planks away from them, and a skirmish developed in which Montoya was hit on the leg with one of the boards. Finally, however, the convicts were subdued and their arms handcuffed behind them. State policemen flanked each of the men and began escorting them into the building. Deputy Warden Montoya stepped in front of the procession, stopping it, and slapped one of the inmates, Billy Battenfield, in the face twice, "screaming at the sub-ject...and saying how he would teach him not to hit an officer," State Police Sergeant Billy Holder told Attorney General investigators. Then Montoya ordered the removal of Battenfield's shoes and proceeded to stomp on the handcuffed inmate's stocking-clad feet, saying, according to a prisoner who witnessed it, "Does that hurt? I'm gonna make sure you do the rest of your time in lockup." A former state policeman, Kenneth Thompson, also witnessed Montoya slap and stomp on two convicts. "Thompson recalled that someone yelled from inside the prison to 'knock it off' because legislators and American Civil Liberties Union lawyers were on tour," the Attorney General's report on the incident said. Thompson also told investigators that "both this incident and another one or two I witnessed involving Bobby Montoya is kind of typical of his attitude toward the prisoners."[7] Montoya denied any wrongdoing, though the Attorney General's report "suggests—but does not conclude—that he tried to cover up his actions and later withheld information from investigators."[8] These findings weren't released until July 31, 1980, but when they were, Montoya's reign inside the Penitentiary of New Mexico ended. Only inside, however. He wasn't fired from the corrections department, only placed on leave, with pay, until another position was found "where the state could continue to utilize his administrative abilities," as the corrections secretary at the time phrased it in the press release.[9]

By Thursday, February 7th, 496 inmates were rehoused in the eight dormitories and three cellhouses that were habitable. Another 470 were transferred to federal and state prisons across the nation, from Leavenworth, Kansas, to Atlanta, Georgia. Those who, like me, had already been granted parole and were doing only waiting time, were to be released before the end of February.

Life in the penitentiary in those first few weeks after the riot was ugly. Those kept in segregation lockup were so outraged by conditions that they set fires and flooded their cells. The men in one of the cellhouses went without water for fifteen hours. Because most of the toilets were smashed during the riot, prisoners had to depend on guards to let them out every time they needed to relieve themselves. But the guards didn't let them out. "To hell with you guys, you wrecked the place," one of the state police officers, there to supplement the dwindled prison staff, heard a guard tell an inmate.[10] Since nature is irresistible, the inmates had no choice but to piss and shit right there on their cellhouse floors. Only when ex-Warden Felix Rodriguez was informed of this did the situation change. He had to order Superintendent of Correctional Security Manuel Koroneos to provide the residents with access to toilets. Thereafter, state policemen escorted one inmate at a time to the bathroom whenever necessary.

Of course, on one count, the guard was right. They had wrecked the place and made it the unsanitary, battle torn shell it was. Whether they deserved to suffer or not was a moot point, because they did suffer as a consequence of their actions. And meals were one of the consequences they suffered. Because the kitchen had been demolished, food was prepared at the National Guard Armory, eleven miles away in Santa Fe, transported to the institution and served to the men in their cells; the same cells where the floors served as toilets. Naturally, the meals were never hot, nor were they served at regular times, a major frustration when the monotony of the day is broken only by food. Until mid-April, that's all there was to do: think and eat. Due to security paranoias and the fact that the visiting room had been wrecked, the administration was allowing each inmate to have only one visit weekly, with one relative, for five minutes. Their short dialogue was conducted at the perimeter fence, the inmate standing in the yard while his visitor stood ten feet away, a moat of land and two cross-wire fences between them. Those locked in Segregation were allowed no visitors until April. Outdoor exercises were stopped until the spring, and there were no indoor exercises to work off aggression, either. The gymnasium had been totally destroyed. Nor were there any education programs to occupy their minds. Most of the education department staff resigned after the riot, and the education wing was badly burned. Some correspondence courses were reinstated in mid-March, but they came in with a whimper, with less than fifty inmates participating. All disciplinary reports, grievances, appeals, and good-time records had been destroyed. This delayed prisoner classification, which affected participation in the few programs that still existed, as well as living-unit status and some parole hearings. Thanks to computers, caseworkers gradually retrieved parole hearing dates and a few other documents, and, together with their own notes and memories, compiled new records on each inmate. Those records would no longer be kept inside the prison but in a trailer outside the main perimeter fence.

There wasn't much mail in or out until mid-April, when the mailroom became operational. What there was of it was often illegally detoured by corrections officers. Correspondence from attorneys is, by Federal Court decree, not to be opened by corrections staff except in the presence of the inmate, and only for the purpose of a search for contraband. "At least one lawyer had his properly marked letter to an inmate client opened and then returned to him without his client's knowledge...A state police officer observed a corrections guard crumple up and throw away an inmate's outgoing letter."[11]

The prison industries program hobbled back to its feet two weeks after the riot, but only eleven inmates were involved in it. Damage to the prison industries building, and vandalism, helped disable the program. According to the Attorney General's report, some of that vandalism was done by "non-inmates [who] stole at least $7500 worth of prison and inmate-owned material from the hobby shop and prison industries."[12] Guards were the probable culprits. Weapons had been found missing from the penitentiary armory at the base of Tower 1 after the riot—five revolvers, a carbine, and a 12-guage shotgun. The shotgun was recovered from a corrections officer after an internal investigation, and one revolver was returned by a former officer as the result of that same investigation. Where the other guns went remained a mystery. It was clear that inmates didn't have them because they never had access to Tower 1 or its keys.

If guards did make off with this property, they no doubt felt justified, given the low pay and dangerous working conditions of the job. Just after the uprising, a group of officers staged a work strike to protest those conditions and the trauma their thirteen co-workers had gone through while being held hostage. On the day the riot ended, these guards handed their own list of demands to corrections officials. Among those demands were: a pay increase to $1,500 per month; additional officers, including a provision that two guards be on duty in each tower for all three shifts; and three weeks of academy training, one week of on-the-job training, and two days of in-service training per month. Though the Legislature put through an emergency bill to raise their pay to $1,000 a month, guards were leaving the penitentiary at a record number. Fifty-six quit after the riot, and interviews conducted by the Attorney General show that eighty percent of the guards employed at the prison six months later would resign if offered a better job. They still complained about cliques, lack of supervision, and fears about their own safety. The large turnover caused the newly organized Corrections Master Plan Advisory Committee to accelerate the recruitment of correctional officers with a large-scale media campaign, an activity that wasn't as successful as hoped: it only attracted twelve of the thirty-four people it needed. Because of this continued shortage of personnel, the administration was still hard-pressed to release guards for training sessions. One August class had to be cancelled because prison officials couldn't spare the men from their duty. Class teachers took the matter into their own hands. They stood at the penitentiary gates when the guards ended their shifts and asked them if any were willing to be trained on their own free time. Twenty-five of them volunteered.

The thirteen guards who had been held hostage during the riot resigned. Eight of them filed legal suits against the state. In a speech in September 1980, prison psychologist Marc Orner said three of these guards were "vegetables" and psychotic due to the riot and others were mentally ill. The guards who were raped were, he said, "totally destroyed as human beings."[13]

The corrections department, too, experienced a turnover in personnel. Corrections Secretary Adolph Saenz, who'd taken the job just two days before the riot, was asked to resign by the governor in June, after being in the position just six months. Some said his ousting was due to the machinations of the corrections clique, but there was equal opinion that he was unqualified for the job and never should have been hired in the first place. There was some merit to this opinion. Saenz had no experience in the field of corrections per se, though he had worked in law enforcement in other countries as an employee of the federal government. Saenz came under fire from prison reform groups after it was learned that from

1965 to 1969, when working as Chief U.S. Officer of Public Safety in Uruguay, he played a role as advisor to Uruguay police, at the time criticized by Amnesty International for torturing political prisoners. In addition, Saenz was censured for creating a new job for his nephew within New Mexico's Department of Corrections, which he supervised. If these things are true, it's a wonder he didn't last. The clique should have welcomed such a *simpatico* game player with open arms. Along with Deputy Warden Montoya, two other members of the corrections clique were ousted from the penitentiary, though not from the department itself. Superintendent of Correctional Security Manuel Koroneous and the hated "Greeneyes," Lieutenant Benito Gonzales, with Montoya, were transferred to the central office of the CDrrections department. According to the Attorney General's report, "The new duties of Montoya, Koroneos, and Gonzales are not clear. One member of the Corrections Department remarked, 'No one knows what they're doing here. We don't know if they're being punished or rewarded. All we know is that they're sitting behind desks collecting hazardous duty pay.'"[14]

Other old-time clique members remained, like prison psychologist Marc Orner. Though his use of the awful plaster body casts, as well as the deplorable condition of psychological services in the penitentiary, had come to the public's attention because of investigations by the American Civil Liberties Union, no one sought to fire Dr. Orner or even to remove him too from the institution. The exposè of his operations wasn't the only slur Orner had weathered either. The Mexican Consul received a letter from him saying that he was seeking to transfer the mentally disturbed Mexican national, Juan Sanchez, to the state hospital "as soon as possible." The strange thing about the letter was that the Consul received it eleven days after Sanchez had been murdered in the riot. The letter itself was dated January 21, 1980, but the envelope was postmarked by the prison meter February 13. There was no chance that it had gotten stuck in the prison mailroom from January 21 through the riot because all mail was destroyed during the uprising. Orner offered no explanation until pressed by a newspaper reporter who had been hounding the Governor for one. Even then, he said nothing himself but filtered his terse response through the prison administrative assistant: it was true he had written the letter, but he didn't recall mailing it. Neither he nor the department could explain the twenty-three day gap between when the letter was dated and when it was sent, which led observers to wonder if Orner had been trying to cover his tracks: the Mexican Consul had been inquiring into Sanchez's treatment in the penitentiary in response to his complaints. When it was discovered that no reservation or request for a bed at the state hospital in Las Vegas, New Mexico, had been made for Sanchez, Orner's action began to smell fishy enough for the Attorney General to conduct an investigation. The report made him smell, if not like a rose, a little better than the wharf. It found that "there was insufficient evidence to support the charge that the letter was written after the riot and made to appear it had been written before the riot."[15] The delay remained unexplained, and Marc Orner remained at his job.

There was one good result of this riot. It forced the legislature to allocate more money to corrections than it had in the past ten years. Better late than never. Fortuitously in session during the uprising, the legislature immediately passed an emergency bill authorizing $87.5 million to be spent on the prison system. Much of this was allocated to rebuilding the wrecked penitentiary into a medium security prison, and to designing a new maximum security facility, for which another $50 million in state bonds was reserved. Funds were also designated for staff salaries and training, and to pay the $2.5 million expenses of the riot. These expenses included $1 million-plus for law enforcement services, $1 million-plus for inmate housing in out-of-state facilities, a $190,406.12 hospital bill, and $500,000 for the investigation and prosecution of the perpetrators of the thirty-three murders, thirty rapes and fifteen heinous assaults that occurred during the riot. As many as 125 inmates could be charged with these crimes, according to the district attorney. In addition, New Mexico could have to pay several more million to the relatives of dead convicts who filed lawsuits against the state. The mother of Joe Madrid, the inmate who died helping others escape from the semi-protection unit, was suing for a million dollars, alleging the state failed to protect her son during the riot. Fifteen inmates filed suits against state officials, asking for $1 million each because they "have permanent physical and mental conditions as a result of gross negligence and failure to take measures which were necessary to prevent the riot," as their lawsuit read. By the time the ninety-day deadline for filing notices of claims expired, there were 412 claims, forerunners to formal suits. Even if the state found a legal loophole and got out of paying settlements, it would still foot the bill for the court's time, its own lawyers, and witnesses. All this time and money because a decade of governors and legislators didn't listen to the warnings and recommendations of grand juries and so-called bleeding heart liberals when they pointed out the faults in the prison system and the ways to correct them.

And still the misery inside the prison went on. Residents claimed that guards were beating them as payback for the riot. On August 22, 1980, an inmate wrote to the Coalition for Prisoners' Rights in Santa Fe:

The only way to stop the beatings is to have someone outside able to be contacted at any time and have permission to enter here at any time with a camera. The public defenders took pictures of the guy that got beat. One white guy had a black eye I couldn't believe. It really hurt me to see him in the Hole...All this bullshit is going to start another riot...There are still a lot of people working here that should not be. Many people feel that the only way to change a prison system...is through violence.

In April, two inmates were stabbed and two beaten in Cellhouse 6, then a maximum-security unit, and two food strikes within a week of each other were staged. In the summer, a New Mexico transferee was critically beaten in an Oklahoma prison by another Penitentiary of New Mexico transferee. In August there was a stabbing at Santa Fe. Both victims were reportedly attacked because they'd helped a guard during the riot. In mid-September, I talked with two inmates who were just released from the penitentiary. They told me things were worse when they left than they had been before the riot. The white and Chicano cliques were fighting each other, and the blacks, who were doubly hated for escaping in the midst of the uprising, were kept segregated from the rest of population. None of the cons were happy with what was going on, and there was talk of another riot. As the transferees began to return from out of state and take up residence once again inside the penitentiary, stabbings and disorder increased. On a Saturday night in September, a group of white inmates in Cellblock 6 took over the unit and demanded to speak with Felix Rodriguez. When Rodriguez, who was acting warden, arrived, they returned to their cells after he promised to talk to each of them individually. He kept his word. He listened to their fears about the safety of the prison until four in the morning, and then again the next day.

Two days before, George Saavedra was found stabbed to death in that same cellblock. No murder weapon was found, though everyone was strip-searched and rooftops and grounds were combed. The stabbing death of Saavedra had set off racial sparks. Chicanos suspected the Anglos in the cellblock of doing the killing, and inmates of both cliques were concerned that the ethnic balance in the living units might get out of kilter and give one group the upper hand over the other. Some inmates were so worried about the violence going on in the institution that a group of thirty-five wrote "emergency letters" to both the *Albuquerque Journal* and Santa Fe attorney Steven Farber, former head of the public defender's office in Santa Fe, pleading for outside intervention to prevent another riot:

> Everyone knows that it's coming down if no one does something to stop it...The administration that is in control of this prison at the present time is

not qualified for the job, and nothing is being done to fix the matter…Right now there is very good reason to believe that there will be another riot. There is tension, anger, resentments. We are constantly being harassed, lied to, the inmates fighting against each other…We plead with you to contact the appropriate people to investigate the administration of the prison…We the undersigned are sending this letter because we fear that a similar situation such as occurred in February 1980 is building up again here at the prison. There is an extreme amount of tension here. We ask you to please not use our names. You know quite well what can happen to us should our names become public or even if this letter should fall into the hands of the administration.[16]

Attorney Farber contacted the civil rights division of the U.S. Department of Justice in Washington on behalf of the prisoners. Arguing that their civil rights were being violated because they were not being kept safe, Farber asked for immediate federal intervention to allay tensions, and for a formal investigation of the way the prison was being run. "If the state can't run that prison, somebody has to," Farber stated.[17] The Justice Department was loathe to jump into state business, however, and did not intervene. They did set in motion a mediation team that was to go into the prison and negotiate a peace between the white and Chicano cliques. From the look of events, they weren't too successful. In October, twenty-one-year old Apolinar Morago was stabbed to death in the recreation yard outside Cellblock 3. His was not a riot-related killing; he didn't arrive at the penitentiary until February 11th. Still, he was killed with vehemence: multiple stab wounds were all over his body. In this case too, no weapons were found, though a thorough search was conducted. What was happening to all the shanks? Members of the Criminal Justice Study Committee wanted to know. They asked penitentiary officials to institute a daily search of inmates working in the prison industries building, where all prison-made knives were created, before they returned to the institution. They suggested that everyone working in prison industries wear distinctive clothing and be strip-searched daily. Having to drop your clothes and stand naked in front of fully clothed guards, while they check out your crevices, is a degrading procedure, especially when done by correctional officers who despise you and probe just a little too deeply. As Senator Manny Aragon reminded the committee, the prisoner's personal dignity should be considered. One of the legislature's more conservative members, who could be counted on to vote against Aragon's many prison reform bills, responded, "Whatever inconvenience the prisoners have is a good trade-off for saving somebody's life. The risk to inmates far exceeds the problem of personal dignity."[18] He didn't understand that the riot was all about personal dignity: it's the lack of personal dignity in prison that makes it dangerous for everyone.

The causes of the February 1980 riot were laid mainly at the doorstep of management. In a speech made to the post-legislative conference of the New Mexico Judiciary on the day his office released the Report of the Attorney General on the February 2 & 3, 1980 Riot at the Penitentiary of New Mexico, Attorney General Jeff Bingaman said:

> I think the first part of our report…demonstrates a pervasive failure of the basics of prison management. Before we can take any further steps, we need to professionalize the security capability of our corrections system…We will discover, I think, by applying a strict and more demanding standard, that while we have experience in our system as measured in years, what we lack is professional corrections expertise.[19]

Would the man the state hired on November 3, 1980 to take over as secretary of corrections be an example of "professional corrections expertise"? The forty-six-year old cigar-smoking ex-warden of the Montana State Prison had a history that made it an even bet one way or the other. He was known in Montana as a guard's warden rather than an inmate's; and in my opinion, it's the latter that's needed in New Mexico. But he wasn't taking over inside the prison. He was going to be the guiding light of the entire corrections network in the state.

There wasn't a lot of difference between Roger Crist's regime in Montana and the conditions at the New Mexico Penitentiary over the past ten years. There were middle-management cliques in Montana, too. One guard, who resigned in 1979, told the Montana Legislature's Select Committee on Prisons that "a clique of officers like street gangs" controlled the daily administration of the pen by keeping the peace with "pressure and violence."[20] Asked what he was going to do about New Mexico's clique, Crist said he wasn't convinced there was one. He'd known Felix Rodriguez for ten years and was expected to rely heavily on his advice. An old-timer at the Santa Fe institution voiced the opinion that Rodriguez recommended Crist for the job because he thought he could control him. Maybe he could, but possibly not. Crist might not be the perfect reformation man, but he did have a reputation for independent thinking and fairness, so there was some hope. In speaking of his work, he said, "When it comes to penology, there are two groups of people, those who want to give inmates lollipops and those who want to sharpen their legs and drive them into the ground."[21] He explained that he falls somewhere in between. He was considered "very fair" by most people who had dealt with him. An Indian woman who served on the Montana Crime Control Commission with Crist felt that he always listened to pro-posals involving minority programs. "Most of the white males on the commission only listened to proposals for guns and flashing lights. Roger would at least evalu-ate community care programs for Indians and other minorities."[22] A University of Montana sociology professor specializing in criminology gave him a mixed review:

> Roger is a little king at that prison [in Montana]. The Supreme Court ruled that it was a violation to censor inmates' mail. So when inmates receive mail that Crist finds objectionable, he doesn't censor it—he just sends it back...A lot of people have come to me and said, "Let's get rid of Roger Crist," but I've never been convinced Roger is the problem. He's done what anybody in that position should do. You put him in the role of a real king, with no controls over him, I don't know what he's going to do. But he just might be able to do the job out there.[23]

Crist's special interest was in constructing new, experimentally designed pris-ons, as he did at the Montana State Prison, a venture that caused critics to accuse him of "empire building." He would be able to build quite an empire in New Mexico. The legislature made $108 million available to create five new institu-tions by 1990. It was disheartening to find out that one of the first appointments he made was to put Deputy Warden Robert Montoya in charge of overseeing construction of these five new facilities. As I write this, Mr. Crist is new and I don't want to create negativity around him before he begins his work. Maybe he will change corrections policy in New Mexico and make the institution more humane, as well as more secure. Maybe the riot has shown the legislature once and for all that they can't turn their backs on the prisons any longer. Maybe everyone in corrections will begin to look for programs to teach, rather than break, a convict.

If I were in charge of designing a new corrections facility, I'd turn the entire system into a "corrections college," a place for the reconditioning and education of everyone who came in, each according to their potential. What was learned in the initial battery of entrance tests would be used to guide the new "student" into one of the many widely diversified courses available. Each living unit would be set up for a particular area of study. For the person geared to intellectual pursuits, we would have an educational facility. Those more inclined to learn a trade would be placed in a vocational unit, not to make license plates but to learn a highly mar-ketable trade. Private enterprise would fund the operation and the trainees would eventually be doing actual work for the company right there in the unit. At that point, the company would pay him a wage, thus keeping the "student" in touch with the everyday realities of the outside world. When you've done ten years earning twenty-five cents an hour, the real world's money scale is mind-boggling. For those more meditatively inclined, there would be a yoga unit, where meditation techniques, yoga, diet, the value of human service, expanding social awareness and a sense of responsibility to the community could be developed. For those artistically endowed, there would be the arts unit, where practice in all art forms would be available, with performance and publication of the work part of the process. In addition there would be a psychological unit where each student, with the help of a counselor as guide, would explore his own psyche and get to know himself better.

Instructors would be the guards: it's easier to train a teacher to be a corrections officer than vice versa. This would be the case in all the units. Staff would be expert or knowledgeable in the field the unit was dealing with as well as the tactics involved in guarding the security of the institution.Training professional instructors to function also as guards would serve to raise the level of corrections personnel within the institution and give the "students" an example of law-abiding citizens that they could not only respect but desire to emulate. In an environment like this, there wouldn't be many security risks; inmates wouldn't be interested in rebelling. As "students" they would have an incentive to stay in line. They'd be learning something that would be of value to them when they got out. They'd look forward to hitting the streets and trying their newfound talents; they'd have hope of keeping their record clean and their asses out of prison.

And did I mention solitary sleeping quarters for everyone? I am now. With doors that lock. It's always comforting to know you can lock your door when sleeping, no matter where you are. In my "corrections college" you wouldn't fear being raped. There would be conjugal visits in my system, not only with one's wife, but with one's girlfriend even if she just became your girlfriend that day.

For the 10 percent who were so hardcore they needed to be locked up in a maximum-security unit, programs would be provided. Yoga in particular has been effective in prison with hard-core dudes and old-timers. "After the first year, we learned that of the thousands of prisoners who wrote to us, most were thirty-five to forty-five years old and had been in prison up to twenty-five years already," a Yoga teacher with the Prison Ashram Project wrote, "or they were people who had been sentenced to two hundred years plus life; people who had less than an eighth-grade education…they were desperately grabbing for something to hold on to; something that could help them remain sane and reopen their hearts that had been closed for so many years because of brutality, distrust and suspicion."[24]

"Prison is a holy place," a Hindu Swami said to me once, and I thought to myself, how naïve this guy is. But later I thought about it. Prison *can* be a holy place; a place a human being can be cured of the diseases plaguing their life. Especially now, when the crime rate is as high as is the incidence of low education and poverty in those convicted of crimes; when the money spent annually per prisoner would buy a year at Harvard; especially under these circumstances would I rush to institute my dream "corrections college" and prove what can be done with a progressive outlook rather than the old eye for an eye.

I can only put my dreams to work on paper, but they really can work if some human being in the field of corrections, or with an active interest in criminal justice problems, will flesh them out inside the brick and mortar. With that hope, I leave you with the wise words of Pope John Paul II:

> The experience of the past and of our own time demonstrates that justice alone is not enough, that it can lead even to the negation of justice and destruction of itself if that deeper power, which is love, is not allowed to shape human life in its various dimensions. In spite of many prejudices, mercy seems particularly necessary for our time.[25]

# APPENDIX

## FOREWORD

1. "Super-Max Punishment in Prisons," Mara Taub, RESIST, Inc. Newsletter 2000/01/: http://resistinc.org/newsletter/issuesr/2000/01/taub/html

2. New Mexico Department of corrections website: http://corrections.state.nm.us./prisons/pnm.htm

3. *Santa Fe Reporter* January 22, 2003 "The Last Stand," Marisa Luisa Tucker

4. Ibid

5. http://accilifeskills.com/cognitiverestructuring/htm/

6. *Washington Times,* "Psyching Out Crime Excuses," Dr. Stanton Samenow, 8/26/04

7. "Dungeons for Dollars—Samenow Fraud," criticism, www. http://globalcircle.net, 199-2000

8. *Santa Fe Reporter,* "The Last Stand," Maria Luisa Tucker, 1/22/03

8a. Ibid

9. Interview with Tilda Sosaya, founder, COPA : Committee On Prison Accountability, an organization of inmate families and friends, 9/2004

10. *Santa Fe Reporter,* "The Last Stand"

11. Ibid

12. Ibid

13. Ibid

14. *Albuquerque Tribune,* "New Mexico Has a Prison Problem," Tilda Sosaya, 8/14/01

15. Letters to families of COPA

16. *American Almanac/The New Federalist,* "Interview: New Mexico Attorney Charges Virginia Supermax 'Concentration Camp,'" Marianna Wertz, 5/29/00

17. Ibid

18. "What is Virginia Doing to People at Wallens Ridge & Red Onion," Amnesty International, www.amnesty.volunteer.org/usa/group159/supermax/html

19. *Crosswinds,* "New Mexico's Iraq Prison Connection," Tilda Sosaya, 6/17/04

20. Ibid.

21. Ibid

22. Ibid

23. *Austin Chronicle,* "Who's Lane McCotter," Michael Ventura, column, 5/28/04

24. *The Nation,* "Exporting America's Prison Problems," Dan Frosch, 5/12/04

*Crosswinds,* "New Mexico's Iraq Prison Connection"

25. *Albuquerque Journal,* 5/14/04

26. *Austin Chronicle,* Michael Ventura Column, 5/18/04

27. *The New Mexican,* "Video Visitation at State Prison," Steve Terrell, 2/20/2001

28. Ibid

29. *The American Heritage Dictionary of the English Language,* Third Edition, Houghton Mifflin Co., 1992

# CHAPTER ONE

1. From the television documentary, "Death in a Southwest prison," ABC-TV, 1980.

# CHAPTER TWO

1. Tom Wicker, *A Time to Die,* New York, Ballantine Books, 1975

2. Michael Serrill and Peter Katel. *Corrections Magazine,* April 1980

3. "Impact," *Albuquerque Journal,* June 10, 1980

# CHAPTER THREE

1. Introduction to George Jackson's *Soledad Brother,* New York, Bantam Books, 1970

2. Thomas Day, "Behind the Wall, A Most Unusual City, *Albuquerque Journal,* May 20, 1974

# CHAPTER FOUR

1. From the television documentary "Hard Time," produced by Dave Bell Associates, Burbank, Ca. 1979

2. Marc Sani, "Prison Perspective," *Albuquerque Journal,* March 30, 1980

# CHAPTER FIVE

1. "Death in a Southwest Prison," ABC-TV, 1980

2. Craig Pyes, *Albuquerque Journal, 1980*

3. Robert Mayer, "The Demon and the Trickster at Play," *Rocky Mountain Magazine*, June 1980

# CHAPTER SIX

1. Jessica Mitford, *Kind and Unusual Punishment,* New York: Random House, 1971

2. "Death in a Southwest Prison," ABC-TV, 1980

2a. *Albuquerque Journal,* September 2, 1975

3. Thomas Day, "Behind the Wall, a Most Unusual City," *Albuquerque Journal,* May 20, 1979

4. Ibid

5. *Albuquerque Journal,* September 2, 1975

6. *Albuquerque Journal,* September 21, 1975

7. Ibid

7a. Report of the Attorney general on the Feb. 2 & 3, 1980 Riot at the Penitentiary of New Mexico ("Report of Attorney General Jeff Bingaman"), September 1980

8. "Death in a Southwest Prison,"ABC-TV, 1980

9. Ibid

10. Report of the Attorney General on the Feb. 2 & 3 1980 Riot, September 1980

11. Ibid

12. Ibid

13. Ibid

14. Ibid

15. Thomas Day, "Behind the Wall, a Most Unusual City"

16. Ibid

17. Ibid

18. Report of the Attorney General on the Feb. 2 & 3, 1980 Riot, 6/80 and 9/80

19. Ibid

20. Ibid

20a. Ibid

21. Craig Pyes, *Albuquerque Journal,* September 23, 1980

22. Ibid

23. Ibid

24. Ibid

25. Ibid

26. Ibid

27. Ibid

28. Ibid

29. Ibid

30. Ibid

31. Ibid

## CHAPTER SEVEN

1. "Death in a Southwest Prison," ABC-TV, 1980

2. M. Serrill and P. Katel, *Corrections Magazine,* April 1980

3. Report of the Attorney General on the Feb. 2&3, 1980 Riot, 6/80

4. Ibid

5. Robert Mayer, "The Demon and the Trickster at·Play in the Bottomless Soul of Man," *Rocky Mountain Magazine,* May/June 1980

6. Ibid

7. Ibid

# CHAPTER EIGHT

1. Jessica Mitford, *Kind and Unusual Punishment,* New York, Random House, 1971

2. Bruce Campbell, "Prison Perspective," *Albuquerque Journal,* March 30, 1980

3. "Death in a Southwest Prison," ABC-TV Documentary, 1980

4. Bruce Campbell, "Prison Perspective," *Albuquerque Journal,* March 30, 1980

5. Ibid

6. Ibid

7. Ibid

9. Report of the Attorney General on the Feb. 2&3, 1980 Riot at the Penitentiary of New Mexico, Part II, September 1980

10. Tom Wicker, *A Time to Die,* New York, Ballantine Books, 1975

11. Jessica Mitford, *Kind and Unusual Punishment*

12. Ibid

13. Tom Wicker, *A Time to Die*

14. Ibid

15. Jessica Mitford, *Kind and Unusual Punishment*

16. Ibid

17. Ibid

18. Ibid

19. Ibid

20. Ibid

21. ibid

22. Theodore Sabin, *The Myth of the Criminal Type*, Connecticut, Wesleyan University Press, 1969

23. *The Challenge of Crime in a Free Society*, Report to the President's Commission of Law Enforcement and Administration of Justice, Washington, D.C., U.S. Government Printing Office, 1967

24. Tom Wicker, *A Time to Die*

# CHAPTER NINE

1. Robert Mayer, "The Demon and the Trickster At Play in the Bottomless Soul of Man," *Rocky Mountain Magazine*, May/June 1980

2. Ibid

3. Report of the Attorney General on the Feb. 2 & 3, 1980 Riot at the Penitentiary of New Mexico—Part 1, June 1980

4. Ibid

5. Ibid

6. Ibid

7. Ibid

8. Ibid

9. Ibid

10. Ibid

11. Ibid

12. Ibid

13. Ibid

14. Ibid

15. *Los Angeles Times,* February 4, 1980

16. Ibid

17. Interview with Senator Aragon

18. Videotape—KNME Public Television, Albuquerque, New Mexico, 1980

19. Ibid

20. Peter Katel, "Riot," *Corrections Magazine,* April 1980

21. Ibid

22. "Death in a Southwest Prison," ABC-TV, 1980

23. Associated Press, Feb. 4, 1980

24. Ibid

25. Report of the Attorney General on the Feb. 2 & 3, 1980 Riot at the Penitentiary of New Mexico, Part 1, June 1980

# CHAPTER TEN

1. Albuquerque Journal, September 24, 1980

2. Lynn Buckingham Villella, "After the Penitentiary Riot," University of New Mexico Alumnus, Fall 1980

3. Ibid

4. "Death In a Southwest Prison," ABC-TV, 1980

5. Los Angeles Times, February 4, 1980

6. Albuquerque Journal, July 31, 1980

7. Ibid

8. Ibid

9. Ibid

10. Report of the Attorney General on the Feb. 2 & 3, 1980 Riot at the Penitentiary of New Mexico, Part 1, June 1980

11. Ibid

12. Ibid

13. San Francisco Chronicle, September 22, 1980

14. Report of the Attorney General on the Feb. 2 & 3, 1980 Riot at the Penitentiary of New Mexico, Part II, September 1980

15. Albuquerque Journal, September 24, 1980

16. Ibid

17. Ibid

18. Albuquerque Journal, October 1, 1980

19. Albuquerque Journal, September 24, 1980

20. Albuquerque Journal, November 1980

21. Ibid

22. Ibid

23. Ibid

24. Interview with Bo Lozoff, "Getting the Word In," Sufi Times

25. Encyclical, December 2 1980

978-0-595-36669-9
0-595-36669-4

Made in the USA
Lexington, KY
25 May 2011